WAT HARIPUÑJAYA

A Study of the Royal Temple of the Buddha's Relic, Lamphun, Thailand

by

Donald K. Swearer

Published by

SCHOLARS PRESS

for

The American Academy of Religion

Distributed by

SCHOLARS PRESS
University of Montana
Missoula, Montana 59801

WAT HARIPUÑJAYA

A Study of the Royal Temple of the Buddha's Relic
Lamphun, Thailand

by

Donald K. Swearer

Library of Congress Cataloging in Publication Data

Swearer, Donald K.   1934-
    Wat Haripuñjaya

    (Studies in religion ; no. 10)
    Bibliography: p.
    Includes index.
    1. Wat Haripuñjaya. 2. Gautama Buddha — Relics.
I. Title. II. Series: American Academy of Religion.
AAR studies in religion ; no. 10.
BQ6337.L352W378   294.3'63   75-33802
ISBN 0-89130-052-X

PRINTED IN THE UNITED STATES OF AMERICA

1 2 3 4 5

Printing Department
University of Montana
Missoula, Montana 59801

WAT HARIPUÑJAYA

A Study of the Royal Temple of
the Buddha's Relic, Lamphun, Thailand

AMERICAN ACADEMY OF RELIGION

STUDIES IN RELIGION

Edited by

Stephen D. Crites

Number 10

WAT HARIPUÑJAYA

A Study of the Royal Temple of the Buddha's Relic,
Lamphun, Thailand

by

Donald K. Swearer

SCHOLARS PRESS
Missoula, Montana 59801

CONTENTS

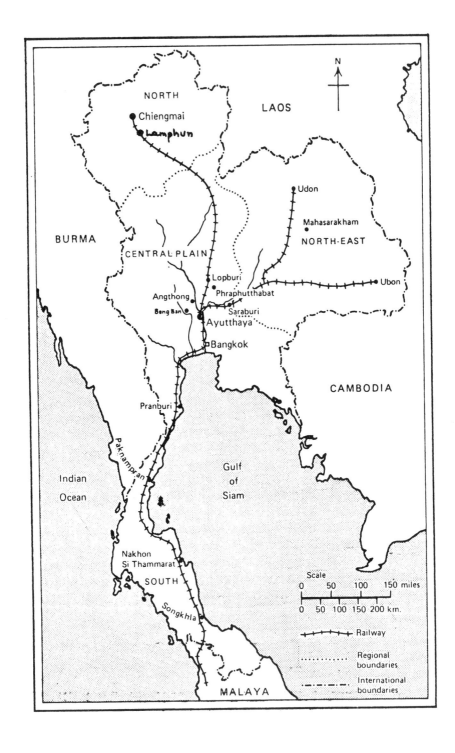

PREFACE

The following study of the Royal Temple-Monastery of the Buddha's Relic (Wat Phra Dhātu Luang Haripuñjaya) in Lamphun, northern Thailand, has a twofold purpose: to illustrate the nature and function of a major Thai provincial *wat*[1] as a place of sacred order and power; and, to provide a specific set of characterizations to the essential relationship that pertains within the various levels or layers into which northern Thai Buddhism can be analyzed. They include most prominently the ontological-moral, the cosmic-natural, and the socio-political. Of these three the first employs the symbol system of Buddhism most explicitly although the other two cannot be fully understood except in the Buddhist interpretative context which informs them. I have utilized hyphenated categories purposely to suggest the range of issues they are intended to cover as well as their open, dynamic, and non-exclusive character. I am keenly aware that too often interpretative schema become static or even absolutized to the point that the phenomena they are trying to interpret seem overshadowed. I devoutly hope that no reader of this monograph will be able to make such a judgment, and that the material will speak for itself in an orderly and meaningful rather than a random manner. It would be naïve to think that our own approach or bias does not shape the data we have at our disposal; however, our obligation as scholars is to fairness and sympathetic objectivity.

This study is indebted to a number of diverse mentors, most of whom remain totally oblivious to the influence they have had on my own eclectic approach to the study of religion. The work of Frank E. Reynolds and S. J. Tambiah has been particularly informative. Reynolds' exceptionally lucid thesis, *Buddhism and Sacred Kingship: A Study in the History of Thai Religion*[2] addresses one of my major interests, the problem of order in the religious and socio-political realms. He does so in bold yet balanced terms and while focusing on Thailand moves through a broad range of time and space. The same central theme of order is picked up by Koson Srisang (*Dhammocracy in Thailand: A Study in Social Ethics as a Hermeneutic of Dhamma*, University of Chicago, 1973) who applies it to modern Thailand from the particular perspective of social ethics.

Tambiah's study of Buddhism in northeast Thailand[3] examines four ritual complexes (i.e., Buddhist ritual, *khwan* rites, cult of the village guardian spirit, rites addressed to the malevolent spirits) both independently and, in respect to their mutual linkage, as a total religious field.[4] While his study is in a different context (i.e., the village) and addresses a particular set of issues (i.e., the relationship between Buddhist and other ritual modes), my own work has been influenced by his professed synchronic/diachronic, structural/functional, integrated or holistic approach.

In addition to Reynolds and Tambiah this study is indebted to the work of Mircea Eliade and Gehardus Van Der Leeuw whose phenomenology is rooted in the structural categories of order and power respectively; to Hans-Dieter Evers whose study of the medieval, Kandyan temple of Lankatilaka raises the important question of the integration of Buddhist, Hindu, and royal value systems; to Richard Gombrich who has shown that what we consider to be normative Buddhism is still a contextual problem; and to Holmes Welch whose study of modern Chinese monasticism is a model of descriptive clarity and a reminder that interpretation should never be substituted for factual adequacy.[5]

The present monograph is the first of a projected trilogy on Buddhism in northern Thailand. The second volume will focus on the distinctive nature of northern Thai Buddhism in terms of its historical development, practice, and teaching. The third volume will be a reader of Buddhist texts translated from the Pāli and northern Thai (Thai Yuan) illustrative of the wide genre of Buddhist literature which became normative in the cultural area known as Lānnā Thai. The total project is, obviously, ambitious and long-term. It will, however, eventually contribute to an awareness of the genuine significance of Lānnā Thai Buddhism which from the mid-fifteenth to the mid-sixteenth centuries was a dominant force in the Theravāda Buddhist world. While a few of the important Lānnā Thai Chronicles were translated by French scholars during the first quarter of this century, little substantive work has been done since then. Some Thai and Western scholars are just beginning serious investigation. Singkha Wannasai of Lamphun and Harold Hundius of the University of Frankfurt have laid the groundwork for a study of northern Thai literature at least equal to that done by Louis Finot for Laos.[6] Other scholars with a major interest in northern Thai Buddhism include Sommai Premchit, Director of the Lānnā Thai Cultural Center, Chiangmai University; Hans Penth, Changmai University; Frank E. Reynolds, the Divinity School, University of Chicago; Charles E. Keyes, Department of Anthropology, University of Washington; Sanguan Chotisukarat who published many books on northern Thai ethnography before his recent death; and A. B. Griswold and Prasert na Nagara whose studies of northern Thai Buddhist sculpture and epigraphy are well known.

In addition to making a contribution to an emerging body of material on Buddhism in northern Thailand, the project intends to serve as an example of a holistic approach to the study of religion. As such it attempts to incorporate historical, functional, and structural perspectives. In this enterprise the author is committed to two propositions: that description and interpretation go hand in hand demanding that a holistic approach employ a variety of methodologies consistent with the multivalent nature of a religious symbol system; and, that the context of the investigation of a religious phenomenon limits (while not determining) the range of appropriate questions that can legitimately be raised about it.[7] Pertaining to the last point it is not accidental but essential that a study of the inter-relationship between ontological-moral, cosmic-natural, and socio-political levels of order in the context of institutional Buddhism focus on an institution of national and regional consequence. Only such an institution can provide the historical depth, range of ritual and festival activities, and the internal and external governing structures adequate to the nature of the problem being studied. In the present monograph the question of the nature and function of the Wat and its relationship to cosmic-natural and socio-political orders will be pursued through the history recorded in several northern Thai Chronicles, a description of the physical plan and art and architecture of the Wat, the Wat as a religious center expressed through its cycle of rituals and festivals, the Wat as a center of both religious and secular education, and, finally, the internal administrative structure of the Wat and its relationship to the order of the Thai Sangha and the Thai state.

I wish to express my appreciation to the National Endowment for the Humanities and the Ford Foundation whose grants made possible my research in northern Thailand during the academic year 1972-1973 and during the summer of 1974; to the National Research Council of Thailand for approving my research in northern Thai Buddhism; to Acharn Singkha Wannasai, my teacher of Northern Thai and Pandit par excellence of Northern Thai culture; to Chao Khun Mōlī, Abbot of Wat Phra Dhātu Luang Haripuñjaya and to Assistant Abbots Phra Khru Prasāt and Phra Khru Sōphon for being so patient with my extended visits; to Acharn Sommai Premchit, project consultant; to Geoff DeGraff for his help in translating the Lamphun Chronicle; to Chao Khun Bodhirangsi of Wat Phan Tong, Chiang Mai, and numerous other monks who provided invaluable insights into the teaching and practice of northern Thai Buddhism; to Francis Seely who shared generously of both his home and his wisdom; to Charles Keyes, one of the best northern Thai ethnographers in the business; to Christine Buffum who typed the manuscript; and to Wattana Wattanaphun for his careful diagram of Wat Haripuñjaya. While it is customary for a list of acknowledgements to end with a note of appreciation to spouse and family, in this case it is made with a particular sense of the sacrifice made by my wife, Nancy, and children, Susan and Stephen, who gave me a summer to complete this manuscript in Chiang Mai while they remained in Pennsylvania.

Acknowledgement is made to the *Journal of the Siam Society* for kind permission to reprint portions of my article, "Myth, Legend and History in the Northern Thai Chronicles" which appear in Chapter I.

Donald K. Swearer
Swarthmore College
September, 1974

¹Whenever possible Thai language terms will be transliterated in their Pāli form, e.g., *ceitya* rather than *cedī*, on the grounds that Western readers will be more familiar with Pāli than Thai. The term, *wat*, underlined when used generically, will be preserved in its Thai rather than its Pāli form (i.e., *vata*, place of religious observance). Pāli transliteration follows the Pāli Text Society *Pāli-English Dictionary*, and Thai transliteration is adapted from Phya Anuman Rajadhon. *The Nature and Development of the Thai Language* (Bangkok: Fine Arts Dept., 1971).

²Doctoral dissertation at the University of Chicago, 1973. Two articles based on the dissertation are: "The Two Wheels of Dhamma," *The Two Wheels of Dhamma*, ed. Bardwell L. Smith, AAR Studies in Religion 3, (Chambersburg: American Academy of Religion, 1972), and "Sacral Kingship and National Development: The Case of Thailand," *Tradition and Change in Theravada Buddhism: Essays on Ceylon and Thailand in the 19th and 20th Centuries*, ed. Bardwell L. Smith, Contributions to Asian Studies, vol. 4, (Leiden: E. J. Brill, 1973).

³S. J. Tambiah, *Buddhism and the Spirit Cults in North-east Thailand* (Cambridge: The University Press, 1970).

⁴*Ibid.*, pp. 337ff.

⁵For example see Mircea Eliade, *Patterns in Comparative Religion*, trans. Rosemary Sheed (Cleveland & New York: World Publishing Co., 1963), Gerhardus Van Der Leeuw, *Religion in Essence and Manifestation*, trans. J. E. Turner (New York: Harper & Row, 1963), Hans-Dieter Evers, *Monks, Priests and Peasants: A Study of Buddhism and Social Structure in Central Ceylon* (Leiden: E. J. Brill, 1972), Richard Gombrich, *Precept and Practice: Traditional Buddhism in the Rural Highlands of Ceylon* (Oxford: Clarendon Press, 1971), Holmes Welch, *The Practice of Chinese Buddhism* (Cambridge: Harvard University Press, 1967).

⁶Louis Finot, "Recherches sur la Litterature Laotienne," *Bulletin de l'ecole Francaise d'extreme orient*, vol. XVII, no. 5 (1917).

⁷I raise the question of the relationship between the context of the study of religion and the range of issues legitimate to that context in a forthcoming article, "The Kandy and Kataragama Äsala Perahäras, Examples of the Juxtaposition of Religious Elements in Ceylon," *Religious Festivals in South Asia*, eds. Guy Welbon and Glenn Yocum.

Chapter I

The Story of the Relic and Its Shrine

Wat Phra Dhātu Luang Haripuñjaya (hereafter referred to by the abbreviated title, Wat Haripuñjaya) is located in the town of Lamphun, northern Thailand, the seat of the government of Lamphun province and the center of the ancient Lava-Mon kingdom of Haripuñjaya whose legendary roots go back to the sixth or seventh century A.D. Lamphun is thirty kilometers distant from the major city in the north, Chiang Mai, formerly an independent Thai kingdom which ruled much of the area from Mengrai's conquest of Haripuñjaya in the mid-thirteenth century to its gradual assimilation from the early nineteenth century onwards into the central Thai kingdom with its capital city in Bangkok. Geographically northern Thailand's mountainous areas are punctuated by fertile valleys planted in paddy rice; ethnically the Thais dominate the valleys of the region but hillside pockets of tribal groups like the Lava, Karen, Yao, and Meo are numerous and only partially assimilated into the Thai nation-state; culturally the region has preserved many unique customs which, in the face of modernization, are all too rapidly dying out.

The history of Wat Haripuñjaya, the major *wat* of Lamphun province and one of the most important *wat*s of the entire northern region, cannot be divorced from either the history of the Kingdom of Haripuñjaya or from the myths and legends surrounding the Wat's relic whose authority rests in the reputed visit of the Buddha to this region. The Wat's relic, in other words, stands as the primary symbol not only of the Wat both as a physical and historical entity, but also of the kingdom throughout its history and, indeed, its pre-history. To appreciate the significance of the Wat and its relationship to the cosmic-natural and socio-political orders, therefore, necessitates a careful examination of the myths and legends surrounding the relic and the founding of Haripuñjaya.

We shall begin with a brief examination of the chronicles studied. Then following a few remarks about the nature of myth and legend, we shall move on to discuss the narrative in terms of its two major strands or layers delineated as the Buddhist and the Brahmanical. In conclusion we shall offer an interpretation of the narrative consistent with the stated purposes of this study.

1

The Texts

Northern Thailand is blessed with an abundance of historical and quasi-historical texts written on palm leaf (*pai lān*) or very heavy paper folded in accordian fashion (*samut khoi*) in northern Thai (Lānnā Thai or Thai Yuan), Pāli or a mixture of northern Thai and Pāli. These northern chronicles or epics are usually identified in Thai as *tamnān* or *phongsāwadān*.The most widely known is the *Jinakālamālīpakaranam* (*Sheaf Garlands of the Epochs of the Conqueror*). A Pāli edition has been printed by the Pāli Text Society of London, and Thai, English, and French translations have also appeared.[1] Even more important for a knowledge of northern Thai Buddhism but less well known outside the relatively small circle of students of Thai history are the *Tamnān Mūlasāsanā* (*Chronicle of the Founding of the Religion*), and the *Phongsāwadān Yonok* (*Yonok Chronicle*), both published in Thai editions.[2] Of more particular focus on the history of Haripuñjaya are the *Cāmadevīwongsa* (*Cāmadevī Chronicle*), and the *Tamnān Lamphun* (*Lamphun Chronicle*).[3]

The most important chronicle for a study of Wat Haripuñjaya *per se* is the *Tamnān Phra Dhātu Haripuñjaya* (*Chronicle of the Haripuñjaya Relic*). Unlike the chronicles mentioned above, the *Chronicle of the Haripuñjaya Relic*, as we would expect, is especially interested in narrating the history of the Wat. It does so moving through the course of sacred Buddhist history beginning with the birth of the Buddha and ending in the mid-fifteenth century at the time of the writing of the chronicle and, coincidently, when the great creative period of northern Thai Buddhism was brought to an end by a Burmese invasion. The Wat Haripuñjaya chronicle, like so many of the *wat* chronicles of northern Thailand, appends to a common body of Theravāda myth, legend, and history a series of episodes of local significance whose historical accuracy is often very difficult to assess. Fortunately, questionable historical veracity need not detract from our main interest, namely the chronicler's efforts to tie together sacred history and secular history, and the well-being of the Wat with the well-being of the kingdom.

Serious, critical investigation of these and similar texts is still in an infant stage. While interesting relationships exist between these chronicles and the chronicle tradition of Śri Lanka and Burma such comparative studies must await the proper editing and translating of the northern Thai texts themselves. Perhaps the most critical work remains Coedès' study of the *Sheaf Garlands of the Epochs of the Conqueror* (hereafter, *Epochs of the Conqueror*) and the *Cāmadevī Chronicle* published around 1925. As David Wyatt of Cornell University and one of the foremost Western scholars of Thai history observes, however, in his review of the recently published *Chiengmai Chronicle* (*Tamnān Phu'n Mu'ang Chiangmai*), "Indeed, this reviewer cannot recall a single major Thai text which has ever been properly edited . . . "[4]

Of the major *tamnān* mentioned there is a disagreement as to which is oldest. Prince Damrong was of the opinion that the *Founding of the Religion* was older than the *Cāmadevī Chronicle.* There are, however, some internal evidences in the *Founding of the Religion* which seem to contradict this judgment. I have discovered at least two instances where the *Founding of the Religion* notes that the same event is interpreted differently in another chronicle, e.g., that Cāmadevī's husband was free to leave Lavapuri for Haripuñjaya because he had become a monk. That particular interpretation is, in fact, found in the *Cāmadevī Chronicle.* Consequently, either the *Cāmadevī Chronicle* is older than the *Founding of the Religion* or utilized an older tradition. We know that the *Cāmadevī Chronicle* was written by Phra Bodhirangsī, the author of *Sidhinganidāna* in the first half of the 15th century. It is thought that the *Founding of the Religion* was begun by Phra Buddhanāna, the 4th abbot of Wat Suan Dok in Chiang Mai (1417-1429) and completed by one of his successors, Phra Buddhapukāma (1489-1499). It would appear that whereas the *Cāmadevī Chronicle* and the *Founding of the Religion* might have been begun at about the same time, the completion of the latter was over fifty years later. It might also be speculated that the narrative style of the *Cāmadevī Chronicle* is closer to an older, oral tradition than the *Founding of the Religion,* which is more descriptive in style. Indeed, on general stylistic grounds there appears to be an evolution from the loose, narrative expositions of the *Cāmadevī Chronicle* to the more descriptive style of the *Founding of the Religion* to the comparatively terse directness of the *Epochs of the Conqueror.*

We know that the *Epochs of the Conqueror* was written by Phra Ratanapañña of the Sinhala Nikāya at Wat Pa Daeng in Chiang Mai between 1516 and 1528 A.D. The *Cāmadevī Chronicle* was written before 1450 and the *Founding of the Religion* before 1500. The *Lamphun Chronicle,* mentioned in the *Epochs of the Conqueror,* refers to the *Founding of the Religion* so, it in turn must have been composed in the latter part of the 15th or early 16th centuries. Finally, the *Chronicle of the Haripuñjaya Relic* is estimated to have been written about 1565. In sum, with the exception of the *Yonok Chronicle,* an acknowledged later composite from several chronicles, the major northern chronicles with which we are familiar were written over a period of a little more than a century between the early 15th to the mid-16th centuries. Roughly speaking, this covers the period from the return of the Buddhist mission to Ceylon in 1430 through the reigns of two of the greatest Buddhist monarchs of the north, Tilokarāja (d. 1487) and Phra Muang Keo (d. 1525).

The content and style of the northern chronicles relevant to the Haripuñjaya story vary greatly. It has been mentioned that stylistically the *Cāmadevī Chronicle* is a loose narrative in a rather florid style, that the *Founding of the Religion* combines narration and description, and that the *Epochs of the Conqueror* is almost entirely descriptive. All three texts are composites of stories and traditions written in Pāli and later translated into northern Thai. While all of the *Cāmadevī Chronicle* and the *Lamphun*

Chronicle are devoted to Haripuñjaya, only about one third of the *Founding of the Religion* and a relatively small section of the *Epochs of the Conqueror* deal with Haripuñjaya. In terms of the range of coverage the *Founding of the Religion* is the most important chronicle, although both the *Cāmadevī Chronicle* and the *Lamphun Chronicle* provide additional valuable information.

Myth, Legend, and History

Before proceeding to an examination of the Haripuñjaya story, a brief, general statement about the nature of myth and legend may be helpful for those few readers who may be unfamiliar with the scholarly use of these terms. Myth and legend are popularly used to denote the opposite of the truth. When we say, "It's a myth" or "He's legendary," we imply that the story or person referred to is false, untrue or exaggerated. Such a popular understanding of myth and legend is at odds with the way in which these terms are understood and used by students of religion and culture. While myths and legends about gods or superhuman beings do not relate stories that are historically or empirically true, they convey archetypal or paradigmatic truth. Thus, a creation myth may include a hierogamy and also function as a model and justification for all human activities including whole complexes of discursive, ethical and ritual systems.[6] We might say simply that the patterns of truth encased in myth and legend infuse the cultures which gave birth to them with higher or transcendent meaning. Myths and legends, consequently, have greater import than factual history for the on-going life of a people. History records what has happened, and while myths and legends may have a relationship to a past history, their permanent significance lies in the fact that they transcend history. Myths and legends may be used to tell us something about the history of a people, but more significantly, they give a commentary on what a people has held and holds to be of lasting value.

The myths and legends surrounding the founding of Haripuñjaya can be divided into two principal segments or layers: the Buddhist, and the *ṛṣi* or Brahmanical. These layers are intermeshed, yet a study of the chronicles reveals them to have been distinct traditions amalgamated into one story. The Buddhist layer is comprised of the Buddha's forecast that his religion would prosper in the area, his visit to Haripuñjaya and the establishment of his relic, and the appearance of his relic during the reign of Ādittarāja (fl. 1047 A.D.). The Brahmanical tradition is comprised of legends concerning the founding of several towns in the north by *ṛṣis* concluding with the founding of Haripuñjaya and the calling of Cāmadevī from Lavapuri (i.e., Lopburi in central Thailand) to act as ruler. The Cāmadevī tradition has the appearance of being a distinct strand in and of itself but since it is woven into the *ṛṣi-*Brahmanical pattern we will treat it in the same way.

The two layers both proceed from the mythic-legendary to the historical or quasi-historical. Thus, the Buddhist strand begins with the mythic-legendary visit of the Buddha to Haripuñjaya, a visit designed to anticipate the reign of Ādittarāja. The *ṛṣis* are legendary cult heroes or clan progenitors who represent not only supernatural power but the creation of civilization or urban culture. They anticipate the Cāmadevī narrative, much of which has the style of legend (e.g., the enumeration of her retinue, the founding of cities along the way from Lopburi to Haripuñjaya), yet she appears on the scene as a historical personage. The most archaic part of the Haripuñjaya story appears to be the *ṛṣi* tradition to which the Cāmadevī layer is appended. The Buddhist strand seems to be a later overlay. In this regard it is significant that the episode of the Buddha's prediction and visit to Haripuñjaya is not related to Cāmadevī but Ādittarāja who ruled some three to four hundred years later. The narrative from Cāmadevī to Ādittarāja definitely has been Buddhasized but the structure of the story does not denote this period as being predominantly Buddhist. From a structural perspective Buddhism comes to the fore only with Ādittarāja.

Our purpose in the following is to tell the story of the founding of Haripuñjaya as compiled from several of the northern Thai chronicles. The chronicles differ to some degree in their accounts. Our intention is not to offer a critical analysis of these differences, but, rather, to present the Buddhist and the Brahmanical narratives noting conflicting reports or other discrepancies only when relevant to the main thrust of the paper. Interpretation will follow the narrative.

The Buddhist Layer

Before beginning the narration of the Buddhist strand of material directly related to Haripuñjaya integrated from the several Chronicles under consideration, it will be worthwhile to see where the *Chronicle of the Haripuñjaya Relic* begins its sacred history and what particular episodes from the Buddha's life are included. The *Chronicle's* narrative ensues with a general reference to the Buddha's previous births as a *bodhisatta* with particular mention of his last rebirth as Vessantara, the prince who personifies the perfection (*pāramitā*) of self-giving (*dāna*). The tale of Vessantara constitutes one of the most popular of all Jātaka tales in northern Thailand and scenes from the legend are often painted on interior temple walls. We shall see in the next chapter that such is the case at Wat Phra Dhatu Haripuñjaya, for example. The recitation of the entire Jātaka lasting over a period of twenty-four hours, still a customary event in northeastern Thailand, is becoming rarer in the north, especially in the immediate vicinity of the city of Chiang Mai.[7] From the Buddha's last *bodhisatta* rebirth as Vessantara the Chronicle follows the traditional chronology of his rebirth in Tusita Heaven, the abode of Indra and Brahma, from where he surveys the world before entering the womb of his mother, Mahāmāya. After his birth, accompanied by appropriate miraculous signs, several traditional events of the Buddha's life up to his first sermon are mentioned, namely: the four sights, the great departure, his observance of an ascetic regime for six years, Sujata's offering, his defeat of Māra, and the first sermon. Two facets of the narrative are of particular interest: the presence of Indra and Brahma, and the careful designation of time. We shall briefly discuss each of these points.

At the occasion of the future Buddha's departure Brahma receives the Buddha's robes and builds a *ceitya* twelve *yōjana* high in honor of the Buddha in Brahmaloka. Similarly, Indra receives his shorn locks and constructs a *ceitya* of equal height in Tāvatimsa Heaven.[8] Furthermore, the *Chronicle* has the Buddha preach the *Dammacakkappavatana Sutta* at the specific invitation of Brahma for the benefit of all mankind.[9] Regarding chronology, each event in the Buddha's life is preceded by a specific time denoted in terms of the lunar calendar and, as we shall see later on in this chapter, in terms of traditional Indian and Burmese calendars. Such a careful designation of time has obvious astrological significance and, together with the rather prominent role of Brahma and Indra, betray a Brahmanical influence. It also might be added that it provides both time and history with an explicit teleology pointing toward the founding of the Haripuñjaya kingdom under Ādittarāja.

The chronicler proceeds with his narration of the Buddha's career through twenty-six Rains Retreats (*vassā pansā*) prior to the Blessed One's visit to northern Thailand. After an extensive description of that episode, the sacred history returns to India and Ceylon before coming back once again to Haripuñjaya and its reputed historic founder, Cāmadevī. The Rains Retreat enumeration functions as a device to demarcate the progress of Buddhism in India, for each *vassā* is associated with a particular place. Moreover, it allows the chronicler to specify particular texts and events which must have been considered especially hallowed or noteworthy at the time of the *Chronicle's* composition. Thus it states that the Buddha preaches the *Vessantara Jātaka* and the *Cariyāpiṭaka*[10] at Kapilavastu; the *Ratana Sutta*[11] at Vesāli, and in his seventh *vassā* he preached the seven books of Abhidhamma in Tāvatimsa Heaven. The miraculous, simultaneous appearance of the five hundred *arahat*s at Kapilavastu now celebrated in the Theravāda world as Mākhapūja is specifically mentioned. Also included in the account is the Nibbāna of Sarīputta and the Buddha, the first three Vinaya councils, Asoka's rule in India, Mahinda's conversion of Śri Lanka, King Milinda's reform of Buddhism, and Buddhaghosa's composition of the *Visudhimagga*. These, then, are the major events outside of the Haripuñjaya story mentioned in the *Chronicle of the Haripuñjaya Relic*.

While the narrator seems to select his materials randomly, he is conveying to his readers both a sense of the most important teachings and events in Buddhist history as well as its measurable direction. In this case the teleology is not governed by the ultimate, ahistorical and, hence, immeasurable goal of Nibbāna, but, rather, the purportedly historical goal of the establishment of a

Buddha-realm in the area of northern Thailand. As we shall see, the Buddha's relic, or perhaps we should say the *ceitya* reliquary, identifies that realm. More importantly, it must be kept in mind that the teleology is brought to fruition by a *cakkavati*, a universal monarch, and not by the Buddha himself. The Buddha's relic is potentially in Haripuñjaya from the time of the Buddha; however, it is only actualized by King Ādittarāja. With this orientation we now turn to the narrative of the Buddha relic.

The Buddha was living in the Isipatāna forest in Benares with his disciples when he looked into the future and predicted that 1008 years after his *parinibbāna* a great city named Haripuñjaya would be established in the country of Sāmadesa or Muang Ping[12] where his religion would prosper. The next day after his morning ablutions the Buddha picked up his begging bowl and flew to Muang Takara (now known as Jaiyabhūmi) where he went on his *piṇḍapata* rounds. The villagers in the area, identified by the *Cāmadevī* and *Yonok Chronicle* as Meng (i.e., Mon)[13] were amazed by his beauty and inquired whether he was a *deva*, *nāga* king, Indra or Brahma. The Buddha then identified himself as the *samma sambuddha*, the savior of the three worlds. After being presented with gifts of food, the Buddha preached to the Mons who then followed him to the future site of Haripuñjaya along the Raming or Mae Ping River.[14]

Arriving at the west bank of the river, the Buddha put down his begging bowl and on the spot a boulder miraculously arose from the ground to prevent the bowl from becoming soiled. The Buddha then predicted that this spot would be the location of his relic to be revealed in Haripuñjaya during the reign of Ādittarāja[15] for the adoration of men and *devas*. In the *Chronicle of the Haripuñjaya Relic* the Buddha is presented with fruit of a betel nut tree by a Lava hunter.[16] After eating, the Buddha cast aside the seed, whereupon it circled three times. The Buddha then interprets this miracle to Ānanda as a sign that at this place Haripuñjaya would be located and upon the place where he sat a golden *ceitya* for several bone relics would be built. Furthermore, he predicts that these relics will appear when the Lava hunter who gave him the fruit of the betel nut tree is reborn as Ādittarāja. When the Buddha had spoken, those who were with him — the *arahat*s, King Asoka, a pink *nāga* king, and the king of the crows all requested a hair relic. He offered one which was encased in an urn and placed in a cave to the south of where he sat.

After his predictions about Haripuñjaya, his relics and Ādittarāja, the Buddha commands his bowl to fly back to Benares. He returns in the same manner and along the way is followed by a white crow who had overheard the Buddha's predictions. The white crow returned to its home in the Himalāyas and ordered his nephew, a black crow, to go to the Mae Ping to guard the holy spot until the advent of Ādittarāja. Also guarding the place were indigenous *devas* (*Founding of the Religion, Lamphun Chronicle*). The *Chronicle of the Haripuñjaya Relic* has the pink *nāga* king and 100,000 of his followers remain to guard the relic and specifically states that the crow was to prevent the sacred site from pollution by animals and people.[17] It should be noted, in concluding this description of the Buddha's visit to the future site of Haripuñjaya, that this episode is part of an extensive visitation by the Buddha to northern Thailand. The *Phra Chao Liep Lōk* (*The Buddha Circumambulates the World*) and other *Buddha tamnān* have both a cosmogonic and etiological import and account for the founding of many towns, *wats* and other holy sites in the north. To my knowledge, the physical presence of the Buddha as represented by his reputed visit to the north is used more extensively to sacralize the land than in other parts of the country.

In the *Yonok Chronicle, Founding the Religion*, and the *Lamphun Chronicle*, the Buddhist layer of the chronicles tied to the Buddha's visit and the Buddha relic is broken by the *ṛṣi* and Cāmadevī traditions. It is resumed again with the advent of Ādittarāja in the year 409 of the Culasakara Era (i.e., 1047 A.D.).[18] Ādittarāja and his queen, Padumavadī, are depicted as devout supporters of the Buddhist Sangha who ruled faithfully according to the Ten Royal Precepts: to provide for the poor, to be established in the five precepts, to make gifts to the Three Gems, to be truthful in word, thought, and deed, to be humble and sympathetic toward others, to be diligent in eradicating demerit, to have pity toward all, not to oppress anyone, to have patience and be restrained, and to be sensitive to the feelings of others.[19]

As expected, the major event in the reign of Ādittarāja is his discovery of the holy relic, related by the chronicler in a most humorous way. After the coronation ceremony in which sixteen Brahmins poured lustral water over the hands of the sovereigns, Ādittarāja retired to his privy to relieve himself. It so happened that these quarters were built directly over the spot where the Buddha relic was being protected by the indigenous guardian of the soil and the black crow. The crow, being warned by the *deva* of the desecration due to take place, quickly flew over the king and let its drippings fall on his head. The king was understandably angered, and when he opened his mouth to call his courtiers, the crow let more of its droppings fall into the king's mouth. So great was Ādittarāja's consternation now that he ordered the entire city to set traps to capture the crow. After catching it, the king was advised by his astrologers not to kill the crow for the bird's strange behavior must portend some important event. That night a *deva* appeared to the king in a dream and told him to have a new-born child live with the black crow for seven years in order to learn the crow's language. This advice was followed and after the alloted time had passed, the child was then able to act as an interpreter between Ādittarāja and the crow. When the king had ascertained the cause of the crow's behavior, he had his privy demolished and the ground reconsecrated. He then prayed, "Servants of the Buddha of the magnificent destiny, Lord, I beg that you deliver all of us, Servants of the Master of the Sages. Lord, make the relic appear to us soon; show to us now this excellent marvel. Render us pure in the merit of our Buddha."[20]

With the above invocation the relic, encased in Asoka's golden urn, appeared and emitted golden rays and perfume. Upon hearing Ādittarāja's intention of moving it to another location, however, the relic disappeared into the earth. In order to recall it Ādittarāja had the entire city cleaned, planted with banana trees and sugar cane, and ornamented with flowers, lamps, incense sticks, and candles. He then invoked the relic to appear again. The chronicler uses this occasion for a recitation of the previous lives of the Buddha: as Phra Sivi he gave his eyes to a blind Brahmin; when the *bodhisatta* was a hare he sacrificed his life so a hungry Brahmin might have food; as a seven year old boy the *bodhisatta* resolved a profound enigma a Brahmin had asked him to explain; and when the *bodhisatta* was an ape he saved a malefactor lost in the forest.[21] This recitation of the Buddha's virtues in previous lives apparently sufficed to lure the relic from its hiding place and the casket rose again paralleling the planet Venus. Ādittarāja then encased Asoka's golden urn in a series of caskets made of silver, bronze, ivory, and finally sandlewood. He then had a *ceitya* constructed and interred the relic during a celebration lasting seven days and nights.[22]

The episode of the discovery of the relic, its appearance, and the preparation for its installation at Haripuñjaya constitute a second founding for the kingdom. As we shall see below the first founding is associated with Queen Cāmadevī and what we are calling the Brahmanical element. Noteworthy in the Ādittarāja story is the pollution/purification polarity; the cleansing of the town; and the use of banana and sugar cane, two essential ingredients in the ceremony performed at times of critical passage to ensure prosperity and long life. The exact significance of the event as a second founding of the kingdom is not entirely clear, i.e., whether Buddhism became established as a state religion at this time. In any event Ādittarāja's espousal of Buddhism as told through the story of the relic was a watershed event in the history of Haripuñjaya and, consequently, is quite properly perceived as a second founding.

The *Lamphun Chronicle* records that twenty-eight sovereigns ruled Haripuñjaya from the time of Ādittarāja to Yība who was conquered by Mengrai in 1281 thereby initiating the Chiang Mai or Lānnā Thai period in the north which lasted until the Burmese conquest in 1556. Even after the Thais, who had pushed south from Yunnan into the Chiang San area north of Chiang Mai, came to dominate the Lamphun-Chiang Mai area, the Wat continued to be a focal point of religious and socio-political consequence. Other important *wats* were built in both Lamphun and Chiang Mai and another famous relic was enshrined at Wat Phra Dhātu on Sutep Mountain, but none of them could completely obscure the luster of Wat Haripuñjaya. The political center of the area shifted to Chiang Mai, to be sure, and new sources of Buddhist thought and practice from Śri Lanka entered; however, if we are to give credence to the chronicle records then the Wat continued to receive royal support and we must assume that Haripuñjaya Buddhism, whatever its exact nature, continued to have a dominant influence until the mid-fifteenth century.[23]

During the period of strong Burmese influence from the mid-sixteenth century until Lānnā Thai was incorporated into central Thailand during the Bangkok Period, Wat Haripuñjaya fell on lean days. The Burmese built many of their own *wats* throughout northern Thailand, one of them being contiguous with the south side of Wat Haripuñjaya. With the freeing of Lānnā Thai from Burmese rule around 1800, the fortunes of the Wat gradually improved. In the modern period, in particular, Wat Haripuñjaya has thrived as a royal temple-monastery: most of the present structures of the Wat have been constructed within the past century; it is one of the three or four major pilgrimage centers in the north; it has become a large educational center; its role as a religious center is rivaled only by the two largest *wats* in Chiang Mai and is not matched by any in Lamphun.

During the five hundred year period from Ādittarāja to the defeat of Lānnā Thai by the Burmese, the names of several monarchs stand out for their support of Buddhism in general and Wat Haripuñjaya in particular. Without going into the broader picture, some details about the kind of support the Wat received and, by implication, the role it played will help us better understand the relationship between the religious and socio-political orders. The following is a partial list of royal beneficence granted the Wat:[24] Sabbasiddhi (c. 1150 A.D.), known through some of the earliest inscriptions as the builder of Wat Mahāwan and the *ceitya* at Wat Kukut, also has a new urn and a *ceitya* built for the relic at Wat Haripuñjaya; Mengrai (c. 1290 A.D.), the founder of Thai rule over Lamphun, covers the top half of the *ceitya* with gold; Kuenā (c. 1350), although most famed for the construction of Wat Phra Yuen and Wat Suan Dok and the receipt of the mission of the Ceylon-trained monk Sumana, greatly expands the size of the Wat; Saen Muang Mā (c. 1400) covers the *ceitya* with 210,000 sheets of gold; Tilokarāja (c. 1440), famed for what the Thais accept as the Eighth Buddhist Council held at Wat Cet Yod, holds a consecration service at Wat Haripuñjaya lasting seven days and constructs Sangha dwellings at the four cardinal points to protect the relic; Phra Muang Kaew (c. 1490) constructs a gold fence around the relic, builds a new *vihāra* and library, gives texts, and donates land. During Phra Muang Kaew's reign the *Epochs of the Conqueror* records that an emissary from the King of Ayudhyā in central Thailand was required to pay homage at the Haripuñjaya relic and that a pact of alliance between the Lānnā Thai kingdom and two Burmese rulers was sealed there.[25] Throughout the centuries Wat Haripuñjaya continued to play an on-going role in sustaining the socio-political integration of an ethnically diverse region and a guarantee of peaceful alliance among neighboring states. The *Chronicle of the Haripuñjaya Relic*, in particular, relates the relic to the peace, prosperity and protection of the land. Indeed, sometimes the Chronicle does not distinguish clearly between the land of the kingdom and the Wat. We shall see in Chapter III that this traditional relationship between the religious realm and the political realm still exists, and that religious and political authority continue to be mutually reinforcing.

There is, to be sure, another side of the story, one in which Sangha and state or religious and secular orders are less harmoniously related. While this story lies beyond the parameters of this study a brief mention needs to be made of its two basic aspects: the centralization of the Thai Kingdom under the reign of King Chulalongkorn which challenged both the political and religious autonomy of the north; the effects of modernization which have accelerated rapidly since the completion of the railroad from Bangkok to Chiang Mai around 1920, and have become particularly acute during the past quarter of a century. The first was the attempt to create a national Sangha at the expense of undermining the northern Thai Buddhist institutional atonomy, ritual practice, and regional religious education control. These principles were codified in the Sangha Administration Act of 1902 which provided for (1) the incorporation of all monks into a national Sangha organization, (2) the establishment of the principle of hierarchical authority centered in a Supreme Patriarch living in Bangkok, (3) the establishment of a national system of clerical education.[26] While this attempt at national religious integration has been largely successful it has not been accomplished without stresses and strains. In short, it would be misleading to see a simple continuity of structural coincidence and functional inter-dependence between Wat Haripuñjaya and the secular order as the latter developed beyond the Thai Yuan region to be included in the modern Thai nation-state.

The second aspect, the impact of modernization and secularization during the past quarter of a century may, in the long run, be the more serious threat to the traditional place of religion in northern Thailand. Already, as we shall see in Chapter III, such important ceremonies as the preaching of the Vessantara Jātaka are beginning to vanish from Chiang Mai, and the attitude of the educated elite, as will be pointed out in Chapter IV, may be developing some incompatibilities with the values ideally upheld in Buddhist education.

The Brahmanical Layer

The founding of Haripuñjaya in the Brahmanical or *r̥si* layer of the chronicles is attributed to a certain sage (*r̥si*) named vasudeva.[27] He appears in the chronicles with either three (*Cāmadevī Chronicle*), or four (*Founding the Religion, Epochs of the Conqueror, Yonok Chronicle*) other *r̥si*s. All of the *r̥si*s are associated with mountains or towns or both: Vāsudeva with Doi Suthep near Chiang Mai, Sukkadanta (or Sukkanta) with Lāvo or Lavo (Lopburi), Anusissa or Anusisaṭa with Sajjanālaya (near Sukhothai), Buddhajatila with Doi Juhapabbata (or Doi Pa Yai, near Lamphun), and Subrahma with Doi Ngām near Lampang. These five high-born clansmen found the teaching of the Buddha attractive and were ordained as monks. Unable to follow the strict rules of the Vinaya, however, they soon reverted to lay life. As the householder life eventually proved unsatisfactory, they became *ṛṣi*s or hermits and acquired the five higher knowledges (*abhiññās*) and five perfections (*sampattīs*).[28]Of these five *ṛṣi*s Vāsudeva is the most important and figures as the founder of several towns including Haripuñjaya. Vāsudeva also plays an important role in the Lava tradition where he is the son of the clan progenitors, or two of the major guardian spirits of the Lava.[29] The Lava were one of the major ethnic groups in the area, and while culturally dominated by the Mon their contribution to the pre-Thai period has been insufficiently investigated.

Vāsudeva always bathed in the Rohinī River or Maenam Khān at the base of Doi Suthep near the present site of Wat Cedī Cet Yod. One day while bathing in the river he saw three sets of male and female infants in the footprints of an elephant, rhinoceros and gayal or bullock.[30] In the *Cāmadevī Chronicle* rendering, Vāsudeva "looks in all directions" and sees children in four footprints (also note that in the *Cāmadevī Chronicle* there are four *ṛṣi*s instead of five): elephant, rhinoceros, bullock and cow (*wua*).[31] Feeling sympathetic for their plight he adopts them and miraculously nurses the children with his fingers. To these six are added yet another couple born of a doe who had conceived by drinking Vāsudeva's urine containing his semen. The *ṛṣi* named the boy Kunāra Rasī and the girl Migapati Rasinī. He married the two when they attained the age of sixteen and made them sovereigns of a city he created named Migasaṅgara. They also ruled over the other children Vāsudeva had raised as well as a large number of hill tribesmen.

Kunāra Rasī and Migapati Rasinī had three sons and one daughter. The eldest son, Kunārikanāda or Kunarishiganāsa, succeeded his father as the ruler of Migasaṅgara. The other two sons were made rulers of two new cities, Anarapura Nagara or Rannapura and Kulissa Nagara.[32] For reasons unstated in the chronicles, Vāsudeva became dissatisfied with the original city, Migasaṅgara Nakhorn, and built a new city to the south of the place where the Buddha had made his prediction and named it Pura Nagara, which was ruled by Kunārikanāda.

Kunārikanāda apparently proved to be an unworthy ruler. The *Founding of the Religion* records that he refused to observe the Ten Royal Precepts and, in particular, refused to mete out justice to a boy who had beaten his elderly mother. She appealed to the *deva*s for help. They heard her plea and said to her, "Old woman, go and tell your relatives and friends to leave the city immediately." After these people had gathered up their belongings and escaped, the *deva*s deluged the city with a great flood destroying everything within it including the wicked king.

Vāsudeva, being informed of the destruction of the city by the *deva*s who protected the world and seeing that the city had, indeed, been entirely annihilated, said, "When I was a *bhikkhu* I realized that people without wisdom and virtue, no matter of what rank or position or number of followers, usually make no progress or self-improvement. Not only are they dangerous to themselves but also cause sorrow to other people. This is the teaching of the Buddha. Now, where can I find a man of wisdom and virtue to rule in accordance with the Ten Royal Precepts?"[33] Deciding that his friend, Sukkadanta in Lavo, could help, Vāsudeva descended from Doi Suthep to seek him out. Coming to the place the Buddha had predicted as the future site of Haripuñjaya, he decided to found the new city there. He sent a message to Sukkadanta via a *deva* who resided in a nearby bamboo grove. Not only did the *deva* bear the message to Sukkadanta but miraculously brought the hermit upstream using the bamboo grove as a raft. Along the way Sukkadanta founded several villages including one where he built a shrine to the *deva* of the bamboo grove.

Vāsudeva and Sukkadanta met at a place half way between Doi Suthep and Muang Lavo which was given the name of Chiang Krung or "half-way city." This spot coincided with the place where the Buddha's begging bowl had been received by the rock. Vāsudeva thrust his staff into the ground and, pulling forth a clump of earth, perceived that the area was rich in precious gems, fuel (charcoal) and paddy rice. If ruled by a man of virtue and justice (*dhamma*), the area would prosper, while an unjust ruler would bring only calamity and famine.

Having decided to found the city of Haripuñjaya at that very location, Vāsudeva consulted with Sukkadanta regarding the city's proper size and shape. Sukkadanta suggested that the city's plan should be based on the sea shell model of Halitavalli Nagara (Sajjanālaya) founded by their friend Anusissa. The two *ṛṣi*s immediately set off for Sajjanālaya where Anusissa promised to find a shell they could use as a design for the borders of their town. Afterwards he instructed a Hasatiling[34] bird to secure a sea shell from the ocean and take it to the two *ṛṣi*s. The bird returned with the shell, perched on the branch of a tree, and let it fall at a spot to the west of where the Buddha had made his prediction. Vāsudeva then took his staff and traced a line around the parameter of the shell. Through his supernatural power, the line became deeper and deeper until it formed the city's moat. Houses and shrines for five kinds of spirits arose from the soil and, for this reason, the city was named Lamphun.[35] Vāsudeva then had the tree *deva*s move their abodes beyond the moat to make the city neat and orderly.

The city being properly prepared, Vāsudeva next sought Sukkadanta's advice about a virtuous and just ruler. "My friend," replied Sukkadanta, "there is a universal monarch (*cakkavatti*) who has succeeded his father as ruler of Muang Lavaratha or Lavo. He has a daughter named Nāng Cāmadevī who practices the five precepts. Let us go and request that she rule our city."[36] Sukkadanta and Gavaya,[37] armed with appropriate gifts and an escort of five hundred retainers, then proceeded to Lavo to request that Cāmadevī become the ruler of Haripuñjaya.

Cāmadevī is depicted in all of the northern chronicles as the daughter of the ruler of Lavo. The *Lamphun Chronicle* adds an interesting footnote to that tradition. There she becomes an incarnation of the fifth wife of Indra born as the daughter of the wife of a village headman. Indra intervenes in an argument over the girl and places her in a 500 petaled lotus. Vāsudeva discovers her one day while searching for food and looks after her in his hermitage until she is two or three years old. His three friends, Sukkadanta, Anusissa and Buddhajalita, admonish him, because adopting a girl is not acceptable behavior for a *ṛṣi*. The four then agree to send Cāmadevī on a raft to Muang Lavo with a note requesting the king to adopt her as his daughter. The *devas* guide the raft safely to the city where the ruler of the city duly accedes to the request of the *ṛṣi*. When Cāmadevī reaches the age of fifteen, the king marries her to his son and together they rule as viceroys in his kingdom. In the *Epochs of the Conqueror*, Cāmadevī's husband is the provincial ruler of the city of Rāmanna, a designation for a Mon area in the central plains of Thailand perhaps extending into Lower Burma.[38]

The chronicles offer a variety of reasons for requesting Cāmadevī to become the ruler of Haripuñjaya. The *Founding of the Religion* and the *Lamphun Chronicle* state that it was impossible to find someone who was virtuous and pious, endowed with the Ten Royal Precepts, and — above all — of royal descent. The *Epochs of the Conqueror* offers another explanation: that the people (of Lamphun) were uncivilized forest dwellers endowed with the characteristics of the animals in whose footprints they were born; that they could not tell right from wrong, good from bad; and that they were unable to govern themselves.[39] Here Cāmadevī is called to rule Haripuñjaya not only because of her reputation for piety and virtue, but also for her connection with the ruling family of the more cultured and powerful kingdom of Lavo. The nature of that connection is ambiguous because of the conflicting testimony of the chronicles.

Sukkadanta and Gavaya from Haripuñjaya are received favorably by the ruler of Muang Lavo. He does not, however, immediately accede to their request but leaves the decision up to Cāmadevī. She, in turn, graciously asks for the king's advice, which is, "To be sent to govern the land towards the sources is of considerable importance, and the request is made by a powerful *ṛṣi*."[40] Cāmadevī consults her husband who is not overly enthusiastic about the proposal even when his father says he can have any other woman in the kingdom for his wife. Yet, in the end, neither Cāmadevī nor her husband can obstruct the wishes of the ruler of Lavo, so she prepares to depart. With her she takes 500 *bhikkhus*, 500 ascetics, 500 scribes, 500 sculptors, 500 jewellers, 500 silversmiths, 500 goldsmiths, 500 blacksmiths, 500 painters, 500 astrologers, 500 governors, and 500 of every other profession to execute every kind of sacred and profane labor. "The *bhikkhus*, ascetics and scribes numbered 1500. On the lists there were 7,000 others, but there were certainly more than 7,000 men, elephants and horses involved. No one made count, and no one knows if the number was in the ten thousands or millions."[41] The king's parting advice was, "My dear daughter, you must realize that you are not an ordinary or common person. You are of royal blood, a descendant of kings. Now you go and become a ruling queen. Take the Buddhist religion and five hundred monks with you which will be the basis for your progress and prosperity. When you are queen, always observe the Ten Royal Precepts for the happiness and prosperity of your people. You must teach your people how to behave according to the Buddha's precepts. The five hundred monks going with you are men of piety and virtue who will protect and pray for you every day and night. Do not deprecate them or be heedless of them."[42]

Cāmadevī departs with her large retinue and along the way builds *ceityas* and several important northern towns including Tak and Hot. Consistent with the sexual-creation symbolism of Vāsudeva's use of a staff to test the appropriateness of the site on which Haripuñjaya was founded, the chronicles have Cāmadevī locate her towns at the spots where her royal archer's arrows fell. One location, Ramayagāma, receives considerable attention in the *Lamphun Chronicle* where it is said that Cāmadevī erected palaces, pavillions and houses all in one day.[43] After some time Haripuñjaya is reached amid the great rejoicing of Vāsudeva and the populace. Cāmadevī is consecrated as queen seated on a heap of gold and "in consequence of it, up to the present day, the name Haripuñjaya has been traditionally handed down for this city."[44] After ruling the city for seven days, Cāmadevī (who had been three months pregnant when she left Muang Lavo) gave birth to two boys, Mahāntayasa and Indavara.

Under Cāmadevī, Haripuñjaya flourished. Monasteries were built for the five hundred monks who came from Muang Lavo and the people piously practiced Buddhism due to the encouragement and example of Cāmadevī. She settled the town according to the regions from which the elements of the populace came: those from Muang Lavo in the northeast; those from Migasaṅgara in the west; those from Ramaniya Nagara in the south; and the interior of the town to the descendants of those born in the footprints of the elephant, rhinoceros and buffalo.[45] She made propitiatory offerings to the town's protective *devas* and requested an elephant of supernatural power so that her sons could protect Haripuñjaya against its enemies. The *devas* granted her request and sent an elephant of silvery white skin and green tusks. Cāmadevī had it duly consecrated on an auspicious day in a ceremony lasting three days and nights. The elephant had such power that everyone who stepped before it was stricken with an illness which could only be cured by making suitable offerings to the animal.

One incident during Cāmadevī's reign receives special attention in both the chronicles as well as the oral traditions of the Lava.[46] There was a Lava (recorded as Lua in the *Lamphun Chronicle*) chieftan named Vilangkha (Milangkha in the *Cāmadevī Chronicle*) who having heard of Cāmadevī's great beauty, wanted her for his wife. He sought her hand in marriage but was refused. The *Lamphun Chronicle* records the conversation between Vilangkha's envoy and Cāmadevī as follows: "Your majesty," said the envoy,

"Vilangkha, who lives in the heights of the Lua mountains, the chief of all the Lua, has sent me with my men to tell you that he would like to have you as his major wife." "O messenger," she replied, "I have never seen your chief. What does he look like?" "Like us," was the answer. "Like you," she cried. "Don't talk of making him my husband. It doesn't seem fit to me that he should even touch my hand!"[47] Vilangkha did not take Cāmadevī's refusal lightly and assembled an army of 80,000 men before the gates of Haripuñjaya. Once again the queen refused the Lava chief's hand in marriage and sent her own troops led by her two sons, Mahāntayasa and Indavara, mounted on the magic elephant. The Lava troops were seized with fright, threw down their arms and headed back for the hills.

The Lava traditions have an expanded version of the Cāmadevī / Vilangkha episode.[48] In response to Vilangkha's pursuit of her hand in marriage, Cāmadevī sets a trial which she considers impossible to accomplish successfully. She tells the Lava chieftain she will marry him if on three tries he can throw his spear from Doi Suthep into the Lamphun city walls. Vilangkha accepts the challenge, and with the first mighty throw almost manages to reach the city wall. Today a small pond marking the spot of the first throw can still be seen. Cāmadevī, now fearful that her ardent suitor will succeed, plots Vilangkha's downfall. Taking her undergarments she fashions a hat for the Lava chief and has it presented as a gift feigning admiration for Vilangkha's great strength. He puts it on his head and launches his second throw only to find that it lands quite short of the mark. His third effort is so weak that the spear is caught by the wind and like a boomerang reverses its direction and pierces Vilangkha's own heart. Unwittingly by wearing the defiled hat, Vilangkha had broken the taboo of touching cloth profaned by menstrual blood. This taboo still conditions relationships between men and women, and accounts for the prohibition against women entering such sacred places as the precinct of the sacred *ceitya* at Wat Phra Dhātu Haripuñjaya in Lamphun or Wat Phra Dhātu Doi Suthep in Chiang Mai.

The *Epochs of the Conqueror* devotes a small paragraph to Cāmadevī herself, being more interested in Lamphun's subsequent history, in particular, wars involving Lamphun, Lopburi, and Cambodia. Cāmadevī's son, Mahāntayasa, was installed as the ruler of Haripuñjaya at the age of seven in an elaborate Brahmanical ceremony including such regalia as a nine-tiered umbrella, jewelled sword and scabbard, and golden slippers. Indavara, not content with the status of *uparāja* under his brother, asked his mother for a kingdom of his own. With the help and advice of the Vāsudeva, Buddhajalita, Subrahman and a hunter, Khelānga, a grand city was miraculously created, named Khelānga Nagara (modern day Lampang), and "on the same day, towns were created as dependencies of the city, a considerable population of all sorts of people was brought into being,"[49] and Indavara was made the ruler.

The Narrative Interpreted

The epic history describing the founding of Haripuñjaya or Lamphun is a series of creation myths and legends in the genre of the Sinhalese chronicles (e.g., *Dīpavamsa*, *Mahāvamsa*), and Indian purānic and āgamic literature which manifested itself in such Pāli works as the *Nidāna-kathā* and the commentary on the *Buddhavamsa*.[50] Above all else, this history narrates the creation of civilization (i.e., Muang, Nagara or town) in the midst of a non-civilization (i.e., forest-dwelling hill tribes). The fundamental polarity of these mythic-legends is, therefore, one between town or city and village or tribe. This polarity is manifested primarily in the calling of Cāmadevī to govern Haripuñjaya, but secondarily in such episodes as Vilangkha's pursuit of Cāmadevī's hand in marriage. Cāmadevī personifies the advanced or Muang culture of Lopburi adumbrated in the stylized lists of professionals in her retinue. She stands in stark contrast to the rustic attributes of those whom she has come to govern symbolized in the *Cāmadevī Chronicle* by the children in the footprints of the forest animals.

On a sociological level, the narrative speaks of the progressive developments of a Muang culture. The first city Vāsudeva created was Migasaṅgara. (*Miga* here should probably not be translated in its particular meaning of deer, but in its generic sense of forest or untamed animal.) Migasaṅgara, then, is a town designating the first settlement of different tribal peoples, yet it cannot be called a civilization or culture at this point. Consequently, other towns emerged until the founding of Haripuñjaya which benefited from its alliance with Lopburi and cultural influences from Cambodia and even Nakorn Si Thammarat.

On a mythological level, Haripuñjaya is what Mircea Eliade would term an *axis mundi* or center of the sacred cosmos. It is in this sense that Vāsudeva descends from Doi Suthep, "looks in all directions," and then takes people from the four cardinal points which serve to populate the cities he creates. Also, the flood destroying Pura Nagara and the sea shell model of Haripuñjaya are intended to convey the emergence of a new, sacred order. A similar mythic mentality informs the narrative of the Buddha's visit and relic. It establishes Haripuñjaya as a place guarded by the *deva*s and the *nāga*s, the cleverest of the birds that fly (crow), the temporal authority of King Asoka, and the spiritual authority of the Buddha himself. Haripuñjaya is a *Buddhadesa*, the center of a sacred cosmos charged with the power of the Buddha's presence conveyed through his personal visit and the deposit of his relic — hence, the chronicler's concern for pollution as evidenced by the role of the crow and the indigenous *deva* as guardians of the reliquary against all kinds of impurities and Ādittarāja's near desecration of the holy spot.

From the standpoint of the narrative's structure as outlined in our description, Lamphun has two foundings, one associated with the *ṛṣi*/Cāmadevī continuum and the other with the Buddha/Ādittarāja continuum. The creation of Muang culture involves the federalization of tribal or communal loyalites through integration into a higher cultural synthesis. Cāmadevī primarily fulfills this function. She symbolizes a new political authority associated with a powerful ruling family of a Muang with a high culture (i.e., Lopburi). Yet, while Cāmadevī brings with her political power invested with the authority of both Buddhism and Brahmanism, the religious identity of tribal affiliation is not yet decisively transformed. Buddhism as the religion of the Muang is not established until the time of Ādittarāja. The Buddha predicts that his religion will flourish in the land of the Mae Ping River at the time of Ādittarāja. There are at least two possible explanations for the chronicler's point — either Buddhism was established in Haripuñjaya by Ādittarā or it began to flourish as a popular religion during his reign. In either case, and the latter may be the most probable, Buddhism was established as the religion of the Muang during the reign of Ādittarāja, not of Cāmadevī. Ādittarāja, then becomes the second founder of Haripuñjaya. No reign matches his importance until that of Mengrai in the 13th century A.D.

The specific details of the narrative are, of course, liable to a variety of interpretations. Some informants say that the black and white crows are meant to symbolize south and north Indian influences; others have attempted to identify the children of the animal footprints with specific tribal groups in northern Thailand; and still others have used Vāsudeva's connection as the son of the clan progenitors of the Lava as a counter to the argument that Haripuñjaya was dominated by the Mons. Such historical exegesis is balanced on the other side by structural interpretations of the narrative as myth. We have already noted the obvious series of binary polarities within that part of the narrative dealing with Ādittarāja's discovery of the Buddha's relic. Also of considerable interest is the interpretation of Cāmadevī-ṛṣi continuum as symbolizing the cosmogonic typology associated with the concept cluster of woman-water-serpent. Such a view takes note of the fact that Cāmadevī was lotus-born, travels by water to Lopburi, and returns pregnant with power to establish civilization in Haripuñjaya; and that, furthermore, the fertile power of woman (i.e., Cāmadevī) is mediated by the asexual ṛṣi.[51]

Our major enterprise, however, has been to offer a particular framework in terms of which to interpret the mythic-legendary founding of Haripuñjaya. I have suggested, by way of summary, that the fundamental polarity in the myths and legends is between civilization (town) and non-civilization (village) and that Haripuñjaya has two foundings, one associated with a ṛṣi tradition[52] actualized by Cāmadevī and another associated with a Buddhist tradition actualized by Ādittarāja. In both cases a new order is being established replete with cosmic symbolism, with obvious socio-political implications, and, in the case of Ādittarāja, decisively articulated in terms of popular Buddhist religion.

[1]Ratannapañña Thera, *Jinākālamālīpakaraṇam* (footnote abbreviation, *JKMP*), ed. A. P. Buddhadatta (London: Luzac & Co., 1962), Ratannapañña Thera, *The Sheaf Garlands of the Epochs of the Conqueror*, trans. N. A. Jayawickrama (London: Luzac & Co., 1968); Ratannapañña Thera, *Jinākālamālīpakarṇa* (Bangkok: Department of Fine Arts, 1968); George Coedès, "Documents sur l'histoire politique du Laos Occidental," *Bulletin de L'Ecole Francaise d'Extreme Orient*, vol. 25, nos. 1 & 2 (1925), pp. 1-202.

[2]*Mūlasāsanā* (footnote abbreviation, MS) (Bangkok: Department of Fine Arts, 1970); *Phongsāwadān Yonok* (footnote abbreviation, *PY*) (Bangkok: Klāng Witayā, 1960).

[3]Bodhirangsi, *Cāmadevīwongsa Phongsāwadān Mu'ang Haripuñjaya* (footnote abbreviation, *CdW*) (Bangkok: Department of Fine Arts, 1967); George Coedès, *op. cit.*; *Chronique de La:p'un* (footnote abbreviation, *TL*), trans. M. Camille Notton, *Annales du Siam*, vol. II (Paris: Charles Lavauzelle, 1930).

[4]David K. Wyatt, "The Chiengmai Chronicle," *Journal of the Siam Society*, vol. LXI, no. 1 (January, 1973), p. 348.

[5]Introduction to Prasert Churat's unpublished English translation of the *Mūlasāsanā*.

[6]Mircea Eliade, *Patterns in Comparative Religion*, p. 412.

[7]The preaching of the *Vessantara Jātaka* will be discussed in Chapter III. The decreasing significance of this event in the Chiang Mai area is one sign of the effect of modernization on traditional religious practice.

[8]*Tamnān Phra Dhātu Haripuñjaya* (footnote abbreviation, *TPDH*), p. 2. The Culāmanī *ceitya* figures prominently in various aspects of northern Thai Buddhist popular piety. It is part of the legend surrounding the renunciation of the Buddha prior to his enlightenment, and is also part of the twelve year life-pilgrimage cycle typical of the northern Thai. This latter issue was discussed by Charles F. Keyes at a meeting of the Northern Thai Society at Chiang Mai University in October, 1973, in a paper entitled, "Buddhist Pilgrimage Centers and the Twelve Year Cycle Northern Thai Moral Orders in Space and Time."

[9]*TPDH*, p. 3.

[10]The *Cariyāpiṭaka* is one of the fifteen books of the *Khuddaka Nikāya*. It relates stories of the Buddha's previous births, especially the ten *pāramī* by which he attained enlightenment. It parallels in verse the last ten prose *Jātaka* stories. See G. P. Malalasekere, *Dictionary of Pāli Proper Names*, vol. 1 (London: Luzac & Co., 1960), p. 859.

[11]The *Ratana Sutta* is one of the *suttas* of the *Khuddakapāṭha* and is also included in the *Sutta Nipāta*. It was included in the *parittā suttas* developed in Śri Lanka which are known in Thai as the *cet tamnān*.

[12]*PY* reads Sāmadesa. *MS* reads Samanta or Muang Ping. Not designated in the *JKMP*.

[13]While there is some disagreement among my informants as to whether Meng is to be interpreted to mean Mon, the weight of the opinion supports this position.

[14]The *PY* elaborates this episode into the conversion of the Mons as disciples of the Buddha. *Phongsāwadan Yonok*, p. 164.

[15]Variant spellings for Ādittarāja are Āditayarāja (*PY*) and Ādicca (*JKMP*).

[16]The chronicles seem to combine two traditions regarding the indigenous population of the Mae Ping region of northern Thailand with some favoring the Mon and others the Lava.

[17]Singkha Wannasai, *Tamnān Phra Dhātu Chao Haripuñjaya* (Chiangmai, 1973), p. 9.

[18]*Epochs of the Conqueror*, p. 106. There is disagreement on the succession of Ādittarāja. In the *MS* his reign is 27th after Cāmadevī; in the *TL* and the *JKMP* it is the 31st. There are even more problems with the chronology. See Coedès, *op. cit.*, p. 25.

[19]This list of virtues is also applied to Cāmadevī. See *TL*, p. 29, *MS*, p. 169. One of the purposes of the chronicles was to offer advice and good counsel to the wielders of political power.

[20]*TL*, p. 48. There are some fascinating binary oppositions in the myth, a point developed somewhat at the conclusion of the monograph.

[21]*TL*, pp. 49-51.

[22]*TL*, p. 57.

[23]In the mid-fifteenth century Haripuñjaya experienced a strong Ceylonese Buddhist influence.

[24]Dates noted are approximate taking into account variation among the chronicles.

[25]*JKMP*, pp. 181-82.

[26]Charles F. Keyes, "Buddhism and National Integration in Thailand," *Journal of Asian Studies*, vol. 30, no. 3 (May, 1971), p. 555.

[27]In the *PY* he appears as Sudeva. While the names of the *rsi*s and the places with which they are associated differ somewhat between the *PY* and *MS*, there are significant differences between the *CdW* and the other two chronicles. It would appear that *CdW* relied on a different source from the other chronicles at this point.

[28]The *JKMP* has Sukkanta becoming a layman again. *Epochs . . .* , p. 97.

[29]Kraisri Nimmanahaeminda provides an interesting account of the conversion of the Lava to Buddhism in, "The Lava Guardian Spirits of Chiengmai," *Journal of the Siam Society*, vol. LV, no. 2 (July, 1967), pp. 185-225.

[30]Jayawickrama's rendering as 'elephant-footed' following the suggestion of Sayadaw U. Titthila has no meaning in terms of the probable cosmological structure of this mythic-legendary event. See *Epochs . . .* , p. 98.

[31]The Thai terms translated here as bullock and cow are *kho* and *wua*. They are formal and common terms for the same kind of animal. It would seem that the author's purpose was to emphasize the four cardinal directions.

[32]The details of this part of the narrative including the names of the cities are quite at variance among the *CdW*, *MS*, *TL*, and *JKMP*. For the most part I shall follow the *MS*.

³³*MS*, p. 140; *TL*, p. 13.

³⁴The Hasatiling, a mythological bird with an elephant head and a bird's body is often used in funeral processions to transport the coffin of an abbot from the Wat to the cremation ground. It signifies the passage from one mode of being to another. Here it symbolizes the creation of a new order of things, the Muang Haripuñjaya.

³⁵*TL*, p. 16.

³⁶*Ibid.*

³⁷*JKMP* has Gavaya going on this mission alone, and the translator queries in a footnote whether Gavaya might be one of the Gavaya-pāda children (*Epochs* . . . , p. 100). Such historicizing of mythic material is very problematical.

³⁸See *Epochs* . . . , p. 100, n. 6. For an analysis of Cāmadevī as a type of cosmogonic paradigm see the concluding section of this chapter.

³⁹*CdW*, p. 26.

⁴⁰*TL*, p. 17.

⁴¹*Ibid.*, p. 19.

⁴²*MS*, p. 153.

⁴³*TL*, p. 25.

⁴⁴*Epochs* . . . , p. 100, n. 8.

⁴⁵*TL*, p. 27; *PY*, p. 170; *MS*, p. 166.

⁴⁶*MS*, p. 169; *PY*, p. 181; *TL*, p. 29. See Kraisri Nimmanahaeminda, "The Romance of Khun Luang Viranga," (mimeographed text).

⁴⁷*TL*, p. 35.

⁴⁸Kraisri Nimmanahaeminda, "The Romance . . . "

⁴⁹*TL*, p. 38.

⁵⁰See E. J. Thomas, *The Life of the Buddha As Legend and History*, 3rd ed. (London: Routledge & Kegan Paul, Ltd., 1949). Thailand's contribution to this tradition is not even noted by Thomas. European scholars are generally unaware of such works as the *Phra Chao Liep Lok* and other northern Thai *Buddha tamnān*.

⁵¹A myth similar to the Cāmadevī story is also found in Campasak. See Charles Archaimbault, "L'histoire de Campasak," *Journal Asiatique*, vol. CCXLIX, no. 4 (1961). A ritual associated with the myth is also analyzed by Archaimbault in *The New Year Ceremony at Basak* (South Laos), trans. Simone B. Boas, Data Paper no. 78, Southeast Asia Program (Ithaca: Cornell University, 1971).

⁵²*Ṛṣis* are persons who have gained supernatural powers through the exercise of ascetic

disciplines. They often play the role of founder and progenitor. See Hermann Kulke, *Cidambaramahātmya* (Wiesbaden: Otto Harrasowitz, 1970) for a suggestion of the role of the *ṛṣis* at Cidambaram, a holy Savite site in South India. Parallels are also found in the Romulus and Remus tradition appended to the founding of Rome. Cf. F. Hermann Strasburger, *Zur Sage von der Grundung Roma* (Heidelberg: Universitäts Verlag, 1968).

Chapter II

The Wat Complex

Wat Phra Dhātu Luang Haripuñjaya is located in the town of Lamphun, the capital and one of five districts or counties within Lamphun Province. The province has a total population of 320,876 of which the town district accounts for 125,567 (1973). The Chiang Mai valley of which Lamphun District is a part is fertile and heavily cultivated. Agriculture is the principal occupation of the people in the province with approximately 90% classified as wet or paddy rice farmers. A wide range of fruits, vegetables and other crops grow in abundance although the *lamyai*, a highly prized northern Thai fruit, is one of the biggest cash earners. Tobacco, garlic, and peanuts are also economically important crops. Flourite mines, shellac production, and a new canning plant provide some light industry, and local handicrafts such as *pāsāng* cotton are sought after.

The town of Lamphun borders the Mae Kuang River which in turn flows into the Mae Nam, one of the major waterways of the Southeast Asian peninsula. Remnants of the old moat and city wall still remain. Even today the modern town lies principally within these walls. Except for a busy main street on which the provincial and district government offices are located as well as the principal shops and the town market, Lamphun appears relatively untouched by the hustle and bustle gradually coming to typify its larger neighbor, Chiang Mai. The Wat itself is bordered by the main road on the west and a stream on the east. Its northern and sourthern boundaries are now formed by small side streets. The entire walled compound of the Wat extends from north to south for approximately 200 yards, and from east to west about 150 yards. Being the town's single largest building complex with lofty *ceitya* spires dominating all other landmarks, the Wat is rivaled in size only by the government compound.

The purpose of this chapter is to examine in some detail the physical structure of the Wat compound itself, its buildings and the way they are organized. While few genuinely old structures remain, several, whether old or relatively modern, hold both an intrinsic and extrinsic interest. More importantly, the plan of the Wat provides a specific example of the orientation and organization of sacred space. While many of the architectural and artistic details are uniquely Thai or northern Thai, the physical structure of the Wat represents, in particular, the cosmological and moral order of Theravāda Buddhism and offers one model for understanding their interaction. Our first task will be to examine the general organization of the Wat in terms of its two basic divisions, the monastic precincts (*Sanghavāsa*) and the public precincts (*Buddhavāsa*). Then we shall look in some detail at the most important structures within the boundary of the *Buddhavāsa*.

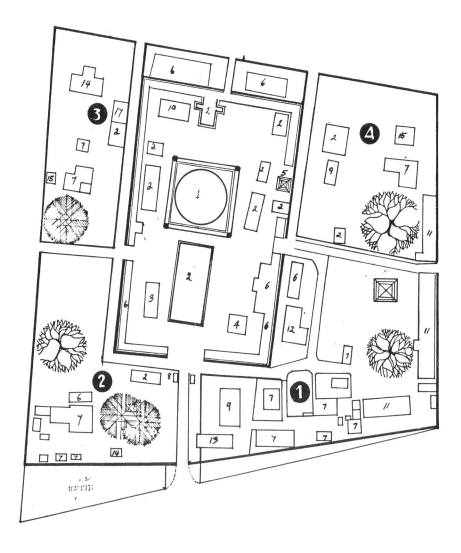

DIAGRAM OF WAT HARIPUÑJAYA

Bold numerals 1-4 designate the four divisions of the Sanghavāsa encompassing the Buddhavāsa. Other structures include the following:

1. Relic *ceitya*

2. Vihāra

3. Library

4. Bell tower

5. *Ceitya*

6. Open verandah

7. Monks' quarters

8. Guardian lions

9. Ordination hall

10. Lamphun museum

11. School buildings

12. Office of the school principal

13. Pond

14. Drum

15. Kitchen

The Plan of the Wat and the Sanghavāsa

The Wat compound is divided into two major areas: one designated especially for the worship[1] of the Buddha by both *bhikkhus* and laymen (the *Buddhavāsa*), and the other specified for the use of the monks, e.g., living quarters, ordination hall (the *Sanghavāsa*). This polarity, nearly unrecognizable in many Thai *wats*, has a respected heritage in the Buddhist tradition. Ancient Buddhist sites in India such as Amarāvati indicate a physical separation between the *ceityas* or centers of public worship and the living quarters of the monks; the Dalada Maligawa or Temple of the Tooth in Kandy, Śri Lanka, is a quarter of a mile distance from the nearest monastic residence; the *ceitya* of the Shwedegon in Rangoon is at a clear remove from the nearby monastic dwellings; and even in Thailand one finds the renovated *ceitya* built on the ancient Buddhist site of Nakorn Pathom ("First City") standing by itself.

At Wat Phra Dhātu Haripuñjaya the distinction between *Buddhavāsa* and *Sanghavāsa* is preserved but less decisively than in the examples cited. As can be seen from the diagram the Wat is, in effect, two walled enclosures, the outer *Sanghavāsa* and the inner *Buddhavāsa* or, more accurately, the Buddha relic enshrined in the *ceitya*. The reliquary stands as the center point or axis surrounded by two concentric circles, the inner, *Buddhavāsa* and the outer *Sanghavāsa*.

Three major types of buildings occupy the *Sanghavāsa*: living quarters, classrooms, and the *uposatha* or ordination hall. The *uposatha* hall, for symbolic reasons alone, must be considered the most sacred, even if functionally not the most significant, of all the structures within the area of the *Sanghavāsa*. The *uposatha* hall or *bot* in Thai generally opens to the east, the direction of the rising sun. It is the only building in the Wat compound set off by *sīma* or boundary stones. Generally these are heavy rounded stones buried in the ground, one under the *uposatha* hall itself and the other eight at the four major and four minor points of the compass surrounding the building. The cosmological orientation of the ordination hall is, therefore, obvious. The *sīma* markers set off the most hallowed building in the Wat, that place where the young man who has reached the age of 20 and having fulfilled the other requisites for ordination[2] is accepted into full membership in a community set apart from the mundane or secular world. It is the only building in the entire Wat compound into which women cannot enter and which is reserved exclusively for the business of the Sangha (*sanghakamma*). One finds that in practice the sacrality of the *uposatha* hall is often not observed, and that it may be used for a dormitory or even a storage building. Such is not the case at Wat Haripuñjaya. The status of the Wat guarantees the care given to the maintenance of the ordination hall; for it serves not only the monks of the local Wat itself but the monks of the entire district. Twice per year, at the beginning of the Rains Retreat on the occasion of Āsālaha Pūjā on the full moon day of July, and at the end of the Rains Retreat on the full moon day of October, all fully ordained monks in the district of Lamphun gather for a joint common recital of the *patimokkha*. In this manner the precedence of the *sīma* of Wat Haripuñjaya over all other *sīma* in the district is annually re-enacted at this most significant time of the monastic year.

Two types of buildings other than the ordination hall characterize the *Sanghavāsa*: living quarters and classrooms. The living quarters are divided into four sections located today rather randomly on the east, north, and south sides. It appears, however, that in times past, each monastic section or division was a distinct *wat* aligned around the periphery of the *Buddhavāsa* at what may have been the minor directions of the compass. This possibility is suggested most strongly at the southeast corner where a *vihāra*[3] and *uposatha* hall are located.

On an average, approximately 25 *bhikkhu*s or fully ordained monks and 70 *sāmaṇera*s or novices reside in the four *Sanghavāsa* sections. Of these the majority will live at the Wat for a period of two to three years. During the Rains Retreat, (*vassā*), as is true throughout Thailand, the number of monks and novices in residence increases temporarily as a result of the Thai custom of having every male spend a brief period as a member of the Sangha.[4] In northern Thailand the number of novices greatly predominates over the number of monks, as is the case at Wat Haripuñjaya, since the period of monastic residence usually occurs in the very early teens and is looked upon as one segment in a boy's overall development and education. This pattern serves to illustrate a point to be made in other connections, namely, that monastic training plays an important symbolic and practical role as an agency of social integration. On the symbolic level formal association with the Sangha is an *a priori* good. To Western eyes *wat* life may appear to be lacking in what Rudolf Otto would have labeled "awe" and "fascination." Yet, having attended a dozen ordination services, I can testify that despite the casualness of *wat* life, there is little doubt that the change of status involved in becoming a monk underlies a profound attitude of respect toward the Sangha.[5] Thus, having been a member of the Sangha is perceived as a good in and of itself. On the practical level, the northern Thai custom of *sāmaṇera* ordination for a period of two or three years instills a knowledge of Buddhist teachings, the ability to participate in the wide and varied ritual life of institutional Buddhism, and — especially if the abbot is a serious teacher — a respect for the virtues of self-discipline and compassion. In short, the novice who spends two years at Wat Haripuñjaya leaves the Sangha more highly regarded because of his association with it and more thoroughly integrated into the customs and moral expectations of his society.

The practical benefit of Sangha membership brings us to the third segment of the structure of the *Sanghavāsa*, namely, education. We shall look in some detail (see Chapter 4) at the various types of instruction carried on at Wat Haripuñjaya. At this point it is sufficient merely to point out that the

Sanghavāsa has a center for those novices and monks who are engaged exclusively in studying subjects relative to Buddhism, e.g., doctrine, history, customs, and language, and another much larger school where a secular curriculum is taught. The latter has one of the largest enrollments in Lamphun and is one of the least costly schools to attend. In this connection it should be noted that as the major *wat* in Lamphun Province, Wat Haripuñjaya, provides a significant amount of subsidy for novices taking traditional Buddhist studies at the Wat. Indeed, on an average, all living and educational expenses are provided for 95-100% of those doing only Buddhist studies and for a sizable number of those combining secular and Buddhist studies. Consequently, the Wat enables boys who could not otherwise afford an education to receive one either appropriate to their status as a monk should they decide on a lifetime career in the Sangha, or to the place they will eventually take in secular life.

The *Sanghavāsa* of Wat Haripuñjaya does not have a meditation center. This may surprise the casual Western student of Buddhism who has understood meditation to be an essential part of the buddhist monastic life. In fact, in Thai Buddhist monastic practice a regular meditation discipline is relatively rare.[6] Some *wat*s are dedicated specifically to the pursuit of Nibbāna, the normative Buddhist goal, through the practice of meditation; however, the great majority of *wat*s provide an environment for the realization of more proximate goals. Consequently, the novice, in particular, spends much more time studying than he does meditating. At Wat Haripuñjaya the abbot takes a personal interest in meditation and leads meditation classes every Sunday and Buddhist sabbath day; however, these sessions are for laymen and laywomen. Novices will receive some instruction in meditation techniques of the *samādhisamatha* variety very much along the lines of Buddhaghosa's *Visuddhimagga*, a well-known and highly regarded text in northern Thailand; nevertheless, the regime of the Wat does not insist on a corporate meditation practice as would have been the case, for example, at large Ch'an or Vinaya temples in China or at Zen monasteries in Japan today.[7]

To summarize: the *Buddhavāsa* and *Sanghavāsa* are the two basic divisions of Wat Haripuñjaya and are oriented around a common center, the *ceitya* reliquary; the *Sanghavāsa*, itself, is divided into four major sections which may have been originally situated at the four minor cardinal directions; the *uposatha* or ordination hall stands as the most sacred structure in the *Sanghavāsa* and is the only building set off by *sīma* or boundary stones; the two schools, one for Buddhist and the other for secular studies, exemplify the Wat's position as an integrator of religious and secular spheres.

The Buddhavāsa

Both the structural and functional center of Wat Haripuñjaya is the

Buddhavāsa. We have already seen how the entire Wat complex focuses on the *ceitya* or reliquary. The cosmological orientation of the Wat's plan receives further reinforcement through the structure of the *ceitya* and the buildings immediately surrounding it. While the style of the *ceitya* reveals cultural influence from Śri Lanka, Burma, and southern Thailand (Śrivijāja), its basic components are tri-partite: the base, the central dome, and the pinnacle or top. This traditional form is often interpreted by Buddhists as symbolizing the Buddha, the Dhamma, and the Sangha; however, cosmologically it represents the three realms (*trai-bhūmi*): the sensuous realm (*kāmadhātu*), the realm of form (*rūpadhātu*) and the formless realm (*arūpadhātu*). This tripartite structure is fundamental to all Buddhist cosmology and received special definition in Thailand in the *Trai-bhūmi Phra Ruang*, a thirteenth century treatise reputed to be one of the first systematically complete Theravāda cosmologies.[8] The *ceitya*, then, in the capacity of an *axis mundi* uniting the three realms, provides a vertical orientation; the four Buddha altars located at the four major directions and four guardian *yaksa*s at the four minor directions around the *ceitya*'s perimeter establish the horizontal orientation. The entire unit, therefore, represents a complete cosmology in both its vertical and horizontal planes held together and empowered by the Buddha-relic at its core.

The *ceitya*-reliquary and its precincts symbolize a 'Buddha-realm' of three tiers or levels of being. The metaphysical dimensions of this tripartite structure evolve in the Mahāyāna tradition into the *tri-kāya* concept or three divisions of the Buddha body applied in a manner equivalent to the *trai-bhūmi* concept to interpret the structure of the *ceitya*.[9] In the Buddhist tradition of northern Thailand, however, the chronicles give the Buddha relic a functional rather than a metaphysical turn. In Chapter I we noted that the imperial power of King Asoka and the magical power of the King of the *nāgas* help guarantee the deposition of the Buddha relics at Haripuñjaya. These three powers associated with the relic are latent until the time of Ādittarāja. A symbiotic relationship exists between the relic and Ādittarāja: by discovering the relics he actualizes their potentiality; but, through the power of the Buddha, King Asoka, and the Nāgarāja inherent in the relic, Ādittarāja is enabled to establish order in the land. The *ceitya*-reliquary together with its legendary background, therefore, links cosmology and history to establish an inviolate order still present despite the erosion brought about through modernization.

One of the oldest and at the same time smallest structures in the Buddhavāsa is a miniature cosmic mountain or Mt. Sumeru (called Sineru in northern Thai) of seven levels atop of which sits the palace (*prāsāda*) of the Lord Śiva who is commonly known in Thai as Phra Isuan.[10] The whole structure rests on a base designed as a *dhammacakka* or wheel of the law. In and of itself the Sumeru is particularly relevant to the symbolism of the *ceitya* because it represents one of the thirty-one spheres into which the tri-partite

Buddhist cosmology is further sub-divided; namely, the Tāvatimsa-bhūmi, the seven tiered abode of thirty-three gods. The Tāvatimsa Heaven holds forth the promise of rebirth in the abode of the gods, a reward for accumulating a store of good merit, and figures prominently in popular fables illustrating the consequences of good and evil actions. Offerings placed on the altar to the east of the Sumeru reflect the hope of the worshipper to be reborn in such a pleasant condition. The *ceitya* symbolizes the entire cosmology from the lowest hell to the highest jhānic (trance) state of neither perception nor non-perception. The Mt. Sumeru, while only one small segment of the entire scheme, draws particular attention because of its special place within the dynamic of kammic rewards. The cosmology, far from being either a rarefied abstraction or unnecessary metaphorical baggage appended to a sophisticated philosophy, is integrally related to both the psychology and ethics of Buddhism.[11] In this sense, the *ceitya* (and the miniature Sumeru) pertains as much to the moral order of the life of the individual as it does to the socio-political order of Haripuñjaya, and the order of the universe. This point will be elaborated in the following discussion of the centers of ritual celebration or *vihāra*.

Several temples or sermon halls (*vihāra*) occupy prominent places within the *Buddhavāsa*. Among them four surround the *ceitya* on the east, west, north, and south. The largest is the main temple (*vihāra luang*), rebuilt in 1918 A.D. after a wind storm stripped off its roof, where almost all *wat* ceremonies and rituals are held including morning and evening services for the monks, sabbath services for the laity, dedicatory services (*ngan chalong*) of various kinds, ordinations into the novitiate, and numerous special meetings. A large altar with three Buddha images, the central image in the meditation (*samādhi*) *mūdra* (hand posture) and two somewhat smaller posterior images in the subduing Māra *mūdra* (*bhūmi-sparsa*), dominate the interior. Paraphernalia for making offerings of incense, flowers, and candles stand in front of the altar which, in addition to the three large images, is crowded with smaller images and miniature Bo trees. A low wide central platform is located in front of the altar and another along the south side occupied by the monks during *wat* ceremonies. The congregation sits on the floor, thereby establishing a sequence of elevations from the Buddha image, to the monks, and finally to the laity. Other than the elaborate altar the most outstanding features of the *vihāra* interior are two pulpits and numerous wall paintings. The pulpits are located on the southwest side, one tall, enclosed northern Thai style pulpit used now only on the occasion of the preaching of the Vassantara Jātaka (the *thet mahāchāt*)[12] during the month of November, and directly beneath it an elaborately carved chair ordinarily used by the abbot or the monk delivering the sermon. Wall paintings, the subject matter of which we shall take up later, cover the top half of both the interior and exterior walls.

During the Rains Retreat from mid-July through mid-October sabbath services or "meetings," as they are called, are held during which a sermon or series of sermons will be preached in central Thai and northern Thai. They will be attended by an average of thirty to fifty older men and women most of whom will spend the entire day and night at the Wat. The meeting begins with the congregation repeating the Three Refuges, "I take refuge in the Buddha, I take refuge in the Dhamma, I take refuge in the Sangha," followed by the Eight Precepts[13] and then chanting by the monks (*suat mantra*) prior to the sermon. Sermons vary greatly both in style and content. They may be read in a prosaic manner from a palm leaf manuscript already listened to several times by the congregation, or, as is the case in the northern Thai style, delivered in a vigorous, chant-like manner. After the service and the noon meal, those who have taken the Eight Precepts may practice meditation either on their own or under the abbot's instruction, talk with their friends, read a book they might have brought with them, or simply nap. Indeed, this custom of spending the sabbath at the *wat* seems not unlike the traditional Western Christian pattern of complete attention to sabbath observance.

To the Western observer the Buddhist sabbath meeting may seem to lack the orderly decorum of a formal Mass or a carefully scheduled Protestant service. While the meeting is underway at Wat Haripuñjaya it is not at all unusual for a stream of visitors to enter the temple at the front and pay their respects to the Buddha through the traditional offerings placed in front of the Buddha images. At the same time others may be outside seated on the wide porches surrounding the *vihāra* carrying on a loud if not boisterous conversation, or some of the children may decide to hit the large gong located on the lawn to the north of the *vihāra*. Through all of this the abbot will be preaching his sermon to the congregation, the men at the front usually in attentive and respectful postures with their hands pressed together in front of them and the women, many of them very elderly, sometimes chatting or perhaps dozing off to sleep. Such looseness reflects both the still largely traditional character of northern Thai society in the Lamphun area as well as the more individualistic nature of Buddhism. Even the Sangha as a corporate body, if compared with monastic bodies in the West, is relatively loosely structured. This observation applies even more to the conduct of the laity at sabbath services. There is little of the rigidity of the typical American Protestant worship service in regard either to schedule or behavior.

Previously we have demonstrated how the *ceitya* as a symbol integrates the authority and power of the Buddha with cosmological and socio-political levels of order. Keeping in mind that the *vihāra* is the place where both worship and instruction take place, we now propose to demonstrate how the art and architecture of the *vihāra* symbolize the integration of the Buddhist moral order with the Buddhist cosmological order. In doing so we will argue that the *ceitya* and the *vihāra* share an identical cosmological structure (i.e., tri-partite) and the same central symbol (i.e., the Buddha in the form of relic and image respectively), thereby providing both a common structure and authority; and, that the *Buddhavāsa* in its totality, or more specifically the *ceitya* and surrounding *vihāra* represent the integration of cosmological, socio-political, and moral orders. In short, whereas in the first chapter we addressed what Koson Srisang refers to as the "hermeneutic of order" in terms of the relationship between myth, legend and history, we now propose to do so through the relationship between the art and architecture of the *vihāra*. Incidentally, we shall learn not an insignificant amount about the content of popular Buddhism.

The walls of each of the four *vihāra* surrounding the *ceitya* are filled with paintings whose themes tell us a great deal about the meaning of popular Buddhism. Of course, these themes do not by any means exhaust the content of popular Buddhism, an analysis of which would involve at least an additional study of frequently delivered sermons and popular tracts. The contents of the paintings do, however, provide us with sufficient information to deduce the primary way the ontic-moral structure of Buddhism is customarily understood and appropriated.

In general the paintings portray either episodes out of the life of the Buddha, *bodhisatta* existence of the Buddha, or tales of *arahats*. The outside walls of the main *vihāra* (*vihāra luang*) depict numerous experiences of the Buddha, e.g., his birth, the great departure, his enlightenment, the preaching of the first sermon, the Mākha Pūjā, and so on. Since these are all more or less familiar they need not be further discussed. The south inside wall of the *vihāra* portrays one representative picture from each of the last ten of the 547 canonical Jātaka tales known in Thai as the *Tosachāt*. The north inside wall is covered with favorite scenes from the last of the Jātakas, the story of Prince Vessantara's acts of self-giving and self-sacrifice rewarded in the end by receiving everything back. This tale is also well known and has recently been discussed elsewhere so does not need further elaboration here.[14] Since, however, the other Jātaka tales are less well known in the West we shall briefly outline their themes.[15] Each will be given according to its formal title and then the name of its central hero:

1. *Muga-pakkha* or *Temiya*, illustrating renunciation. Temiya, *bodhisatta* and only son of the King of Benares, overhears his father sentencing four robbers to terrible punishments. Knowing that such actions lead to rebirth in hell for 80,000 years and that he normally would have to succeed to this position and perform similar actions, Temiya feigns the role of a crippled mute. Quite disturbed, his parents devise all kinds of trials such as withholding food, putting him in a burning hut, having serpents coil around him, but through all of them he remains silent and motionless. Finally, all else failing, the *bodhisatta* is condemned to be killed and buried. Thus released from his obligation to follow as king after his father he reveals his *bodhisatta* form and assumes the life of an ascetic. His example inspires his parents who follow after his example and are thus also released from the punishment of hell.

2. *Mahājanaka*, illustrating perseverence. Mahājanaka is the son of the King of Mithila who was killed by his brother before Mahājanaka's birth. At

her husband's death the queen escapes to the city of Kalacampa with the help of Sakka. There a kindly Brahman takes her in. At the age of sixteen, Mahājanaka, teased by his friends about his paternity, is told the story of his father's death and resolves to regain the kingdom. He boards a ship for Suvannabhūmi but after seven days the ship sinks. Through many trials and tribulations Mahājanaka perseveres until at last Manimekhala, the guardian of the sea, helps rescue him. The *bodhisatta* is then chosen as the King of Mithila only to realize that possessions bring only sorrow. He becomes an ascetic eventually to be reborn in the Brahma heaven.

3. *Suvannasāma* or *Sāma*, illustrating loving-kindness. Sāma is the son miraculously given to Dukulaka and Parika, an ascetic couple living in penance for an evil deed done by their father many lifetimes ago. When Sāma is sixteen his parents lose their eyesight so he faithfully looks after their every need. So gentle is he that even the deer befriend him. One evening while drawing water from a pond he is shot with a poisoned arrow by the King of Benares. This event proves to be ultimately restorative for through the King's remorse his evil deed is forgiven; through Sāma's parents' suffering and grief their penance is ended; and through their cleansing tears Sāma is restored to life.

4. *Nemi*, illustrating resolution. Nemi is the last king in the Makhadeva line, all of his predecessors having, in old age, entered upon the ascetic life and attained to Brahma's heaven. Nemi becomes renowned for his righteousness and generosity but is not satisfied with himself. He cannot resolve the question, is it more fruitful to lead a holy life or be faithful in almsgiving. The gods in Tāvatimsa heaven are so pleased with Nemi that they send Matali the charioteer to bring him to them. On the way he passes through various hells and heavens, before reaching the abode of Sakka. After seven days he returns to describe to his people the punishments for those who do evil and the rewards for those who do good.

The pattern of the Nemi tale is better known in Thailand in the guise of Phra Mālai, the virtuous *arahat* who, like Nemi, visits the Buddhist hells and sees first-hand the kinds of punishments reserved for those who take life, steal, commit adultery, lie, or drink intoxicating beverages, and the various kinds of heavenly beings one becomes for doing good deeds. The story of Phra Mālai's visit to see those being punished for wrongdoing is one of the most popular sermons in northern Thailand (*Phra Malai Pot*), often preached as a funeral oration; and the tale of Phra Mālai's visit to Tāvatamsi heaven where he discourses with Indra (Sakka) and meets Meitreya, the future Buddha, is customarily preached at the beginning of the *thet mahachāt*. Mural paintings from the Phra Mālai cover the interior walls of the *vihāra* to the west of the *ceitya* known as the Than-chai Vihāra.

5. *Maha-ummagga* or *Mahosodha*, illustrating wisdom. The Mahosodha is a long and involved Jātaka designed to show the knowledge of Mahosodha, the fifth and most brilliant sage of King Videha of Mithila. The tale includes

many tests of wit, such as the time Mahosodha adjudicates the claim two women make for the same child by having each take the child by a hand and a foot and try to pull him over a line. When the child cries out in pain the real mother lets go. The major episode, however, involves Mahosodha's ability first to circumvent Brahmadatta's plot to conquer King Videha and then to reconcile the two. The murals on the interior walls of the Buddha Vihāra to the south of the main temple are scenes from the Mahosodha.

6. *Bhuridatta*, illustrating moral virtue. The *bodhisatta* is born as Bhuridatta, son of a *naga* king. Wishing to attain the abode of Sakka he keeps the moral precepts and fasts upon the top of an ant hill every day. Eventually he is captured by a Brahmin who breaks every bone in his body so he can perform in village market places. There he is discovered by one of his brothers and step-sister and through a miraculous event is set free. Bhuridatta's faithfulness to the moral precepts eventually wins for him the reward he sought.

7. *Canda*, illustrating forbearance. Canda, the son of the King of Pupphavati, is appointed judge by his father in place of the Brahmin, Kandahāla, who has become corrupt. Later Kandahāla convinces the king to sacrifice Canda and all his possessions as the way to gain heaven. At the moment Canda is about to be sacrificed Sakka intervenes, Kandahāla is killed by the crowd, and Canda is crowned king.

8. *Mahānāradakassapa* or *Nārada*, illustrating equanimity. Angati, the King of Videha, is convinced by the ascetic Guna that he need not fulfill his responsibilities of almsgiving toward others in order to gain heaven, that there are no other worlds, and no consequences of evil deeds. At the request of Rujā, Angati's daughter, the *bodhisatta*, Nārada, appears before the king and convinces him to resume his responsibilities toward his realm and to lead a life of self-restraint and equanimity.

9. *Vidhurapandita*, illustrating truth. In this tale the *bodhisatta* is born as Vidhurapandita, the wise counsel of the king of Indrapatta. He is taken to the realm of the Nāgas by Punnaka, a *yakkha* (demon) general. Through a series of stratagems, misunderstandings, and miraculous happenings, Vidhurapandita finally converts the *naga*s and *yakkha*s to the truth and all are reborn in the Brahma world.

10. *Vessantara*, illustrating self-giving (see Chapter 3).

Each of these tales intends to teach a virtue, a special virtue perfectly embodied in a particular hero. Often the main point of the Jātaka is obscured in the vast amount of detail incorporated into the story, yet the moral is never completely lost. Vessantara is the last *bodhisatta* rebirth before Gotama, the Buddha. As such the pattern of his life most nearly approximates the pattern of the Buddha's life. The Buddha as the *sammasambuddha*, the complete and totally enlightened one, embodies all of the perfections encapsulated in his previous ten *bodhisatta* lives. The *Tosachāt* reflect the multiple aspects of the perfections of the Buddha just as a prism reflects the separate colors composing light. Many of these same perfections are also embodied in the paintings of the *Tīkā Phāhung*[16] found on the walls of the fourth *vihāra*, the Phra Lavo Vihāra.The stories illustrated in mural form on the *vihāra* walls at Wat Haripuñjaya, therefore, reflect a moral totality, unity, and perfection parallel to the cosmic totality symbolized in the structure of the *Buddhavāsa*. The "content" of the *vihāra*, as it were, depicted in the life of the Buddha as Siddhattha and in his ten previous lives, conveys a moral perfection which, when embodied by a layman, leads to the reward of a heavenly existence. Conversely, their opposing qualities lead to rebirth in the Buddhist hells. These proximate states, removed from and yet — unlike Nibbāna — depictable in concrete terms, cannot be separated from the tri-partite universe symbolized in the *ceitya*. Indeed, the tri-partite roof architecture of the *vihāra* serves to reenforce even further the connection between the Buddhist moral and cosmological orders.

The tiered roof of the Thai temple stands out as its most distinctive architectural feature. I would like to advance the hypothesis, consistent with the point of view of this study, that this feature provides an important comment on the development of popular Buddhism, that in particular it represents a move from the *ceitya* to the *vihāra* as the focal point of public worship but that it does so while preserving the basic tri-partite structure of the *ceitya*. No one could disagree that in Thai Buddhism the *vihāra* dominates the religious life of the people. Yet, as evidence both within and outside of Thailand indicates, popular Buddhism from the time of Asoka onwards focused on the *ceitya* by itself. We know from Ajānta and elsewhere that *ceitya*s came to be enclosed in caves and eventually in buildings, and that Buddha images of one type or another were often associated with them. In northern Thailand, for example, such old temples as Wat Pa Daeng in Chiang Mai, still retain the feature of an interior Buddha *ceitya* or *mandop*. As the congregational life of the *wat* came to dominate monastic life the separate *Sanghavāsa* disappeared, as we have already seen, and the *ceitya* came to be consistently located outside of the *vihāra* as its importance for public worship declined relative to the *vihāra*. The *vihāra*, as the place where the *bhikkhu*s chanted and the laity was instructed in the Buddhist way of life, emerged as the principal functioning center of the *wat*; moreover, as is the case at Wat Haripuñjaya, the tri-leveled roof style retained the basic tri-partite cosmological structure originally symbolized by the *ceitya*.

Our proposed interpretation may be summarized as follows: within the *Buddhavāsa* the *ceitya*-reliquary and four surrounding *vihāra*s are the central nexus; this nexus, as the womb of the Buddha's relic brought to life by Ādittarāja, demonstrates the coincidence between the cosmological order and socio-political order; the *vihāra*, as the worship and teaching center, demonstrates the inter-relationship between the cosmological and moral orders; and the entire complex represents an integrated cosmological, socio-political and moral universe.[17]

[1]Worship is a term fraught with ambiguities. Some educated Buddhists object to the use of the term, worship, on the grounds that the Buddha is not deified and, therefore, not worshipped in the sense that the Western Christian or Jew worships God. The simplest forms of Buddhist worship consist of paying respects or honoring the Buddha by bowing before the Buddha image and making offering of flowers, incense, and candles.

[2]Such as being free of debt and healthy in mind and body.

[3]The Pāli term, *vihāra*, traditionally referred to the habitation of the *bhikkhu* or meeting place for monks. In Thai Buddhism the *vihāra* (Thai: *wihān*) typically refers to that building where monks conduct morning and evening meetings and where sabbath services are held.

[4]Jane Bunnag (*Buddhist Monk, Buddhist Layman. A Study of Urban Monastic Organization in Central Thailand*, Cambridge: The University Press, 1973) and others who have studied Buddhism in central Thailand have observed a very significant increase in monastic membership during the Rains Retreats due to the practice of taking *upasampadā* (ordination) for one *vassā* (Rains Retreat). While this custom is becoming more characteristic of northern Thai practice as well, the traditional practice of a two to three year ordination into the novitiate still largely prevails. Consequently, relative to central Thailand the north has a larger ratio of novices to monks.

[5]See Jane Bunnag, *op. cit.*, Chap. II, for varying attitudes of the laity toward monks, and the reasons for some of these attitudes.

[6]See Jane Bunnag, *op. cit.*, pp. 53-54, for corroboration in central Thai monastic practice.

[7]For example, see Holmes Welch, *The Practice of Chinese Buddhism, 1900-1950* (Cambridge: Harvard University Press, 1967); D. T. Suzuki, *The Training of the Zen Buddhist Monk* (New York: University Books, 1965).

[8]Phrayā Lithai, *Trai Bhūmi Phra Ruang* (Bangkok: Khlang Withayā, 1972). An English translation with extensive notes is being completed by Mani and Frank Reynolds and will be published by the Stanford University Press (see *Buddhist Text Information*, no. 1 (November 1974).

[9]The Lama Anagarika Govinda has a fascinating discussion of the symbolism of the *ceitya* in Tibetan Buddhism in *Foundations of Tibetan Mysticism* (London: Rider & Co., 1969).

[10]The fact that Śiva rather than Indra sits astride this Mt. Sumeru undoubtedly testifies to Khmer influence.

[11]Winston L. King has a helpful discussion of Buddhist cosmology in *A Thousand Lives Away: Buddhism in Contemporary Burma* (Cambridge: Harvard University Press, 1964), Chap. III.

[12]Literally, "the preaching of the great rebirth." See Phya Anuman Rajadhon, *Thet Mahā Chāt* (Bangkok: Fine Arts Dept., 1968).

[13]The eight precepts are: refrain from destroying life; refrain from taking what is not given; refrain from breaking celibacy; refrain from false speech; refrain from distilled and fermented intoxicants; refrain from taking food after noon; refrain from seeing shows, dances, entertainments, and from adorning or perfuming one's body; refrain from sleeping on a soft or luxurious bed. See Khantipalo, *Buddhism Explained, With Special Reference to Thailand* (Bangkok: Social Association Press, 1968), pp. 87-97.

[14]See S. J. Tambiah, *Buddhism and the Spirit Cults* . . . , pp. 160-68.

[15]Elizabeth Lyons, *The Tosachāt in Thai Painting* (Bangkok: Fine Arts Dept., 1971); Elizabeth Wray, et al., *Ten Lives of the Buddha: Siamese Temple Paintings and Jataka Tales* (New York & Tokyo: Weatherhill, 1972); *The Jātaka or Stories of the Buddha's Former Births*, trans. E. B. Cowell and W. H. D. Rouse (Cambridge: Harvard University Press, 1907).

[16]*Tīkā Chayamangkhala Aṭṭhaka Desanā* (*Phāhung*) (Bangkok: Liang Chiang, 1951).

[17]My argument here which sees the symbolism of the *vihāra* combining Buddhist and pre-Buddhist elements in one organic structure is consistent with the general outlines of Southeast Asian *ceitya* (*stupa*) theory advanced in a variety of ways by Paul Mus, Georges Coedès, and H. G. Quaritch Wales.

Chapter III

The Wat as a Religious Center

The *wat* in Thailand serves a number of different functions. Anthropologists have observed that it plays the role of orphanage, bank, old-folks' home, museum, playground and so on.[1] While the *wat* does, indeed, perform these roles it is, nevertheless, first and foremost a religious center. Worship and celebration are the major purposes of the *wat* and the main rationale of its existence, and are expressed primarily in the ritual and festival cycle. The rituals and festivals celebrated at the *wat* may be analyzed from several different perspectives. They can, for example, be structured according to their calendric occurrence on a daily, weekly, monthly, annually, or only occasional basis. Such a structure has the advantage of presenting the religious year as it evolves chronologically for both monk and layman. A second and related way would be to divide the ritual/festival year into seasons, i.e., monsoon season, hot season, cool season, coincident with the agricultural cycle. A third way would be to divide rituals and festivals into two groups: those perceived primarily in terms of merit-making (*tam pun*), literally "doing merit," and those with limited merit-making potential. For example, ceremonies where gifts are presented to the Sangha are perceived primarily in terms of merit-making whereas simple attendance at sabbath services is rationalized primarily as something a good Buddhist should do rather than primarily as making merit. A fourth way and one more coincident with the thrust of this monograph, is to see how the ritual and festival cycle integrates the Buddhist or moral-ontological, cosmic-natural, and socio-political realms. To a certain degree each of these realms can be seen as distinct; to an even greater degree, however, they are integrated into a single religious expression which we might more accurately label Thai religion rather than Thai Buddhism.[2] Partially for this reason, I have chosen broad rubrics connoting orientations rather than more specific, denotative categories like Brahmanism and magical-animism. Before proceeding with our analysis of the Wat as a religious center a few introductory and somewhat random observations are called for.

First, it should be kept in mind that our discussion of rituals and festivals is not intended to be exhaustive. In particular little or no attention will be paid to ceremonies outside of the Wat where monks may participate on a regular basis, e.g., weddings and house dedications. Secondly, the funeral, the major life-cycle ritual to take place at the Wat (although it may also occur in the home) is omitted from our discussion on the grounds that it is outside the central focus of the paper. Thirdly, any analysis of religious festivals from whatever perspective should not ignore the pure entertainment value of such occasions. In other words, no theory should be taken to be so comprehensive that religious festivals cannot be seen for their carnival aspect. Fourthly, in terms of attendance at Wat rituals and festivals, a relatively small cadre of older and financially stable adults will generally be seen supporting the great majority of events at Wat Haripuñjaya and other *wats* in the town. Since they are often retired they have the time to devote to such occasions and being reasonably well-off they can afford to make the necessary donations. In addition to this nucleus, many of whom are on the Wat Committee known as the *kammakan Wat* (see Chapter 5), more irregularly defined groups will participate in sabbath services, ordinations, and annual festivals. The last, as we would expect, draw huge crowds with many young people in attendance. Finally, it should be noted that the term "ritual" applies to celebrations customarily held inside the temple (*vihāra*) on a variety of calendric schedules while the term "festival" is used for annual ceremonies where much of the activity occurs outside the *vihāra* proper and where large numbers of people are usually in attendance.

The Buddhist Orientation

The cycles of rituals and festivals whose frame of conscious interpretation is primarily Buddhist dominates the religious life of Wat Haripuñjaya. Most of these events occur at the level of the *Buddhavāsa*; however, on the level of the *Sanghavāsa* two highly visible ritual occasions take place in the *uposatha* hall: ordinations (*upasampadā*) and the *patimokkha*, the twice monthly recitation of the *bhikkhu* confessional and the 227 Vinaya rules. Of these two rituals the *patimokkha* is exclusively for *bhikkhu*s whereas ordinations involve the laity to an important degree. Indeed, one of the most merit-consequential events to take place in the Wat is the ordination. It is a curious paradox of being one of the most solemn and Nibbānically oriented of Wat ceremonies and, yet, at the same time excells all others in the degree it can affect one's place in the world calculated according to one's *kamma*. I emphasize this point since I do not believe that in the practice of northern Thai Buddhism the apparently logical contradiction of Nibbānic and kammic goals integrated into the same event leads to cognitive conflict.[3]

Ordination is an acting out of two events closely connected in the consciousness of most Buddhists in northern Thailand: the renunciations of Prince Vessantara and of Prince Siddhattha.[4] While the nuances are different both events symbolize the concept of *dāna*, self-giving or self-sacrifice. In the case of Prince Vessantara *dāna* is seen as a good in itself and, much like the example of Abraham, living up to this ideal is rewarded by the Prince receiving back what he had surrendered. In the case of the Siddhattha *dāna* becomes a necessary perfection (*pāramitā*) on the way to a higher end, namely, Nibbāna. Ordination in northern Thailand and, indeed, in other Theravāda Buddhist countries, can profitably be perceived as synthesizing the models of both Vessantara and Siddhattha. That is, in ordination the family gives up its most prized gift — a son. The son, in theory at least, seeks Nibbāna, the goal reached by Siddhattha. In doing so, however, he produces virtue or merit both for himself and his parents which is most often calculated in material rather than moral or ontological terms. In this sense ordination emulates Vessantara more closely than Siddhattha. This synthesizing of models was reflected by one informant who stated that the princely costume worn prior to ordination as a novice symbolized either Prince Vessantara or Prince Siddhattha.

Ordination and the Vinaya recitation, the two most important ritual events of the *Sanghavāsa*, dramatize episodes in the life of the Buddha and his community. The Buddhist orientation to rituals and festivals at Wat Haripuñjaya stems from these two models: the life of the founder and the early monastic community. Consequently, as is true also in the Christian and Jewish liturgical years, rituals and festivals serve to contemporize events thought of as historical and associated with the foundation of the tradition. In this way present day followers of the Buddha participate in a sacred time which is both historical and ahistorical, particular and universal.

Whereas the ritual of ordination is modeled after the renunciation of the Buddha, the *patimokkha* is modeled after the example of the early community. Sukumar Dutt has shown how the custom of the twice monthly *bhikkhu* confessional was adapted from earlier Brahmanical practice and how it evolved within the early Buddhist community itself from a simple confession of faith in the Buddha's Dhamma, to the mutual agreement to a binding set of relatively simple rules, and finally to a ritual occasion.[5] As practiced at Wat Haripuñjaya the *patimokkha* is a ritualistic recitation of the 227 Vinaya rules by one of the senior monks at the Wat. All *bhikkhus* of the Wat are required to be in attendance or to have officially excused themselves for appropriate reasons, e.g., illness. Even though they do not recite the rules themselves, their silence, in theory, registers their consent. As pointed out in Chapter 2, at the beginning and end of the Rains Retreat (*vassā*) all *bhikkhus* within the jurisdiction of the Lamphun town district join in a common *patimokkha*. This custom registers the common unity of the monks in the district in the Buddha's Dhamma and Vinaya but, more significantly, the precedence of Wat Haripuñjaya over all other *wats*.

Vassā, the three-month period of Rains Retreat falling between July and October, stands as the most hallowed season of the Buddhist year, especially for members of the *bhikkhu-sangha*. This tradition stemming from the time of the Buddha is reputed to have been instituted because of the difficulty of mendicancy during the monsoon rains and may have eventually extended to the establishment of permanent monastic dwellings.[6] As presently maintained at Wat Haripuñjaya and other northern Thai *wats*, *vassā* represents a time of relatively intensive study and meditation for those monks and novices who are permanent members of the Wat, as well as for those who reside there for a single Rains Retreat, a custom still in vogue. At Wat Haripuñjaya this peak period is marked by two ceremonies at the beginning and end of *vassā* known in Thai simply as "entering *vassā*" (*khaw pansā*) and "leaving *vassā*" (*ǫǫk pansā*). The collective *patimokkha* at the Wat *uposatha* hall for all Lamphun District monks bracketing the Rains Retreat also sets this period of time apart, as does the Āsālaha Pūjā at the beginning (see below), and the ceremonies presenting the monks with new robes (*kathiṇa*) the following month. Indeed, the month of *kathiṇa* festivities is gradually becoming one of the most popular merit-making seasons of the entire Buddhist calendar, as wealthy lay patrons vie to sponsor ever more elaborate modes of gift giving to the Sangha.[7]

The ceremony for the monks and novices at Wat Haripuñjaya held the evening after the full-moon sabbath day (i.e., *Āsālaha Pūjā*) reenacts this time-honored tradition attributed to the Buddha himself. The ritual, however, is much more than a mere reenactment of a paradigmatic event. Known as a service of forgiveness (*kǫ khamakan*) it is a recitation of the teachings of the *Sārāṇiyadhamma Sutta* followed by a formal request for forgiveness on the part of all monks so that this period of more restrictive residence may be carried on in harmony and without grudges. The teachings of the Sutta have an important functional value, ideally helping to engender positive and helpful attitudes and actions among the monastic community:

> Let your actions be motivated by good will towards monks and novices before and behind you; endeavor to help others especially when they are ill.
> Let your speech be governed by goodwill in speaking to monks and novices . . . especially in teaching others.
> Let your heart be filled with goodwill towards monks and novices and think only of things useful to others.
> Divide fairly the gifts that you receive with the other monks and novices; do not put aside things for yourself.
> Observe the precepts in purity equally with the monks and novices so you will not be a cause of offense to others.
> Let your opinions be in harmony with those of others; do not quarrel with others because you differ with them in viewpoint.[8]

There are, to be sure, other ceremonial occasions exclusively or largely entailing the Sangha. In general, they are directed toward advancement in the Sangha either through education or ecclesiastical promotion. Such events fall under the rubric of *chalǫng* or dedications. For example, Wat Haripuñjaya now has an annual ceremony where monks and novices who have passed various levels of Pāli examination are honored. Celebrated in a new hall which bears the name ,"Dhamma study hall," the ceremony is attended by senior monks from throughout the province and important government officials. In addition to chanting (*suat mon*) which engenders every auspicious occasion with the proper powers, and gifts of new robes and books for the monks and novices being honored, there are speeches by the abbot of the Wat, the head of the Pāli school, a lay member of the Wat Committee, and a senior provincial government official. Further discussion of the significance of these two types of Sangha ceremonies will be taken up in the chapters dealing with the Wat as an educational and administrative center.

Buddhavāsa rituals and festivals occur throughout the year, some on regular, others on an irregular basis. The weekly sabbath service (*wan phra*) previously mentioned is celebrated throughout the year although customarily sermons are delivered only during the Rains Retreat. Whenever a new building is constructed or a Buddha image installed an appropriately elaborate dedicatory ceremony will be held. Such occasions are, of course, irregular. On a regular, and usually annual basis, there are several minor ceremonies, such as the commemoration of the Buddha's cremation or his descent from Tāvatimsa heaven after preaching to his mother. However, the major ceremonies associated with the Buddhist year in particular are *Visākha Pūjā* in remembrance of the birth, enlightenment and Nibbāna of the Buddha; *Mākha Pūjā* commemorating the coming together of the 1250 *arahat*s to worship the Buddha at Veluvana Vihāra; *Āsālaha Pūjā* signifying the beginning of the Buddhist religion, i.e., the Buddha's first discourse at the Deer Park in Benares; the beginning and end of the Rains Retreat (*vassā*); and, the preaching of the *Vessantara Jātaka*.[9] All of these ceremonies are associated with events in the lifetime of the Buddha. We find, therefore, a consistent emphasis on the *person* of the Buddha in the realm of sacred history (ch. 1), in the organization and construction of the Wat (ch. 2), and now in the ritual/festival cycle of the Wat. The inference drawn from these three aspects of our study of Wat Haripuñjaya leads to the conclusion that the Buddha establishes reality whether in terms of ordering the land, its history, or its cycle of communal celebration.

Visākha Pūjā brings together the three principal events in the life of the Buddha — birth, enlightenment, and death — all reputed to have occurred on the same day. Consequently, this celebration receives more attention than any of the others. It takes place during the full moon day of *Visākha*, the sixth month, which falls in April or May. Most years *Visākha Pūjā* at Wat Haripuñjaya falls at the same time as the Wat's annual festival, a coincidence which enhances the meaning of both events. The day being the full moon sabbath as well as *Visākha Pūjā*, celebration begins with crowds of lay men and women coming to the Wat to present food to the monks (*tak pāt*). The remaining activities during the day are taken up largely with the Wat's annual festival and it is only in the evening that the *Visākha Pūjā* really begins. At about dusk crowds of lay people from Lamphun follow a contingent of monks and novices from the Wat in a three-fold clockwise circumambulation around the *ceitya*-reliquary. In their hands the participants hold a lighted candle and

incense and as they wind their way slowly around this sacred axis clouds of
incense fill the air. Before the procession started they would have been
admonished by the abbot or one of his assistants to reflect on the meaning of
the Buddha's birth, enlightenment, and death. One author writing about the
seriousness with which such recollection should be taken commented that
these three events must be lifted out of the realm of mere factual history about
the life of the Buddha. It should be remembered, he continues, that the
Buddha made greater efforts than anyone before or after him for the goodness
and beauty of the world; that his enlightenment represents the highest truth
ever attained; and that his *parinibbāna* guaranteed that his merit would never
be exhausted.[10]

After the circumambulation interpreted as symbolizing the three events
incorporated into *Visākha Pūjā*, the Three Gems (Buddha, Dhamma,
Sangha) or the *tri-sarana* (*anicca, dukkha, anatta*), the crowd then fills all of
the four major *vihāra*s of the *Buddhavāsa* for an all night session of preaching
and chanting. A traditional *visākha* sermon composed of twenty-nine sections
may be preached on this occasion. Because the intent of this chapter is to show
in what ways one cycle of Wat rituals establish an orientation around the
Buddha and his early community it will be worthwhile to outline the progress
of this sermon, the *Pathamasamphoti*. The text proceeds as follows: 1) the
wedding of Suddhodana and Mahāmaya, the Buddha's parents; 2) the
Buddha in Tusita heaven, beseeched by the gods to help mankind, enters the
womb of Mahāmaya; 3) the birth of the Buddha and the miraculous
appearance on the same day of his future wife, Yasodhara, his beloved
disciple, Ānanda, his horse, Channa, and his charioteer, Kanthaka, and the
Bo tree; 4) two predictions by Brahmans, one that he will be either a world-
ruler or a Buddha, and the other that he is destined to become a fully
enlightened one because he possesses the thirty-two marks of the great man
(*mahāpurusa*); 5) the Buddha is given the name, Siddhattha; his mother dies
after seven days; Siddhattha marries Yasodhara at age sixteen; 6) the four
encounters, aged person, sick person, corpse, mendicant, prompt the Buddha
to follow the mendicant path; 7) Siddhattha follows an ascetic way, e.g.,
abstaining from food, restraining his breath, for six years, then adopts a
middle path as more appropriate to mind development; his five followers
desert him; 8) Sujātā makes a food offering to the Buddha thinking he is a tree
devata; the Buddha's begging bowl miraculously moves upstream as a sign he
will become enlightened; the Buddha determines not to move from his seat
under the Bo tree until he realizes his highest goal; 9) Māra and his forces
attack the Buddha; he successfully wards them off by calling Nāng Thoranī[11]
to witness on his behalf; Nāng Thoranī drowns the forces of Māra by wringing
out the water from her hair that she had collected every time the Buddha
performed an act of *dāna*; 10) attainments immediately prior to
enlightment — the eight trance states, knowledge of the previous conditions
of all men, clairvoyance, the cycle of Dependent Co-origination (*paticca-*

samuppāda); the Buddha's enlightenment; 11) the Buddha spends seven days each at seven places after his enlightenment, e.g., the Bo tree, the location where he surveys the Abhidhamma, the place where Mucalinda, the Nāgarāja, protects him from the rain, the spot where Indra and his first two lay followers make offerings; 12) the Buddha worries whether the people will be able to understand his teaching; the gods of Brahmaloka perceive his concern and send devatas to assure him that there are groups among humankind less blinded by attachment than others who will be able to comprehend his message; 13) the Buddha preaches the first sermon (Dhamma-cakkappavattana Sutta); 14) the five former followers of the Buddha to whom his first teaching was given become arahats; more people become disciples; 15) the Buddha's activities in Uruvela; the Buddha impresses Bimbasara of Rajagrha; 16) Sāriputra and Moggalāna become followers of the Buddha; 17) Suddhodana requests the Buddha to come to Kapilavastu; his people become the Buddha's disciples; 18) Yasodhara's sorrow over her husband's rejection of the princely role; 19) Devadatta, the Buddha's cousin, attempts to kill the Buddha and then to split the Sangha; he is punished by the earth swollowing him up; 20) the Buddha predicts the future coming of Meitreya and tells Ānanda that the bhikkhu with the lowest seniority will be the next reborn as Meitreya; 21) the Buddha heals his father's illness and he becomes an arahat before his death; an order of nuns is established on Ānanda's request but not equal to that of the bhikkhu-sangha; 22) the Buddha performs several miracles but forbids his disciples to do so without seeking permission; 23) the Buddha travels to Tāvatamsa heaven and preaches the Abhidhamma to his mother; 24) the Buddha descends from Tāvatamsa heaven on a crystal ladder given by Indra; the Buddha goes to the top of Mt. Sumeru where he performs a miracle witnessed by all from the Pretaloka to the Brahmaloka; 25) the death of Sāriputra and Moggallāna; 26) the Buddha's parinibbāna; 27) the Buddha's funeral; collecting the Buddha relics; the rulers of the major petty kingdoms of northern India come to request relics; 28) Mahākassapa buries the remainder of the relics which are not unearthed until the time of Asoka who divides them among various cities in India; 29) reasons for the decline of Buddhism in India.[12]

We can see from the above outline that the Pathamasamphoti reviews the major events in the life of the Buddha and the early Buddhist Sangha. While fewer lay men and women are inclined to endure an entire night of preaching and chanting than is reputed to have been the case in the past, a large number of people do remain. Of course, they are not listening attentively all of the time and many nap; nevertheless, those who stay perceive the act as a discipline for the body and the mind. Indeed, it is!

The text itself, or similar texts if this one is not used, is a composite of canonical and popular-commentary traditions. Its rehearsal highlights those timeless events in the life of the Buddha which depict him as a teacher-miracle worker. He is superior to the gods for they serve him, the goddess of the earth for she testifies to his reigning virtue, to the *Nāgaraja* who protects him, and to the monarchs who follow his teachings and solicit his relics. *Visākha Pūjā* is "Buddha's Day," and often goes by that name. It is the celebration in honor of the first of the Three Gems, the cornerstone of the Buddhist Way. Much more than a founder-teacher, he appears in the celebration of *Visākha Pūjā* as the tamer of men and gods whose universal power expresses itself in the particular events of a legendary history remembered, if not relived, at a time, auspiciously enough, just prior to the monsoon rains. More on that point later, however.

Āsālaha Pūjā, a second major celebration directly associated with the Buddhist cycle, remembers the *Dhammacakkappavattana Sutta*, the "First Sermon" delivered by the Buddha at the Benares Deer Park. Consequently, *Āsālaha Pūjā* symbolizes for Buddhists the following: the proclamation of the Buddha's teaching and, hence, the birth of their religion; the beginning of the Sangha, i.e., the conversion of Koṇadanna and the four ascetics who later attained arahatship after hearing the second discourse (the *Anattalakhana Sutta* or The Characteristics of Not-Self), and were ordained with the Buddha's words, "*Ehi bhikkhu*" (Come, monk!); and, finally, *Āsālaha Pūjā* represents the completion of the Three Gems (Buddha, Dhamma, Sangha).[13]

Coming in the eighth month (*Āsālaha* refers to the eighth month of the lunar calendar which usually falls in July), *Āsālaha Pūjā* is celebrated on the full-moon sabbath day (*wan paen*) at the beginning of the Rains Retreat (*vassā*). Instituted as a legal and religious holiday in Thailand in 1958 (B.E. 2501), its coincidence with *vassā* enhances the significance of this most important season of the monastic year. At Wat Haripuñjaya the day begins as the *Visākha* celebration with food presented to the monks and novices at the Wat. Afterwards, the *patimokkha* is recited by all fully ordained monks in the district of Lamphun (see above), followed by a series of sabbath related events including a series of sermons in central and northern Thai. In the afternoon a procession bringing an enormous Rains Retreat candle (reputed to be large enough to burn throughout the entire three months!), sent to the royal Wat by the king, winds its way from the nearby compound of government buildings to the Wat where it is installed in the *vihāra*. The focus of the event, circumambulation around the *ceitya*-reliquary, is very much like *Visākha Pūjā* with preparatory instructions by the abbot or a senior monk who then leads the large crowd of people holding lighted candles and incense in the *wien tien* (circumambulating with candles). Following the circumambulation, monks, novices, and laity enter the *vihāra* for the *Āsālaha Pūjā* service which is supposed to include the chanting of the *Dhammacakkappavattana Sutta*, a sermon expositing it, and chanting in the *suat saraphanna* style, a special, highly intoned mode of chant.

On the cognitive level *Āsālaha Pūjā*'s exposition of the Dhamma in straightforward, discursive terms compliments *Visākha Pūjā*'s picture of the Buddha replete with the vivid metaphor of Theravāda commentary. The first and second discourses of the Buddha need not be rehearsed here other than to note that they encapsulate the core of early Buddhist teaching, the Four Noble Truths and Eightfold Noble Path, with particular emphasis on being freed from any attachment to an ignorant misunderstanding of the self. Furthermore, the suggested adoration upon the presentation of incense, candles, and flowers before the Buddha image makes particular note of the teaching considered most basic to Buddhism, "what comes into existence must pass out of existence." (i.e., *anicca*).[14] Coming as it does at the beginning of the Rains Retreat, a period of more serious study for monk, novice, and laity, *Āsālaha Pūjā* seemingly discards the myth and legend for philosophy, a particular ideology accepted as being an accurate description of the way things really are. In short, coupled with the new reality represented by the Buddha goes an understanding of that reality as revealed or taught by him. Thai Buddhists see *Visākha* and *Āsālaha Pūjā* together completing the Three Gems. In a similar vein I would interpret them as representing a fusion between the primary symbol or point of orientation in the Buddhist cycle (the Buddha), the universal truth (Dhamma) embodied by the Buddha's teaching, and the monastic order which mediates both the Buddha and his teaching to the world. Here we might profitably draw a parallel with the relic as the center of the Haripuñjaya kingdom, the ideal of a Buddha-realm (*Buddha-desa*), and the Cakkavattin as mediator of the ideal.

While the above suggested set of relationships constitutes a ritual totality on what Richard Gombrich would label both affective and cognitive levels,[15] the two ceremonies we have discussed are not, in themselves, a closed circle. That is, other ritual occasions highlight particular events in the cycle, e.g., the Buddha's cremation, preaching the Abhidhamma in Tāvatimsa heaven, etc. *Mākha Pūjā*, after *Visākha* and *Āsālaha Pūjā*, is the most important of these occasions. *Mākha Pūjā*,celebrated on the full-moon sabbath (*wan paen*) of the month, usually falls in the middle of the third lunar month, that is mid-February. It remembers four "miracles": 1250 *arahat*s gathered together to worship the Buddha at the Veluvana Mahāvihara in Rājagrha; all had received ordination from the Buddha with the words, "*Ehi bhikkhu*"; none had received prior notification but miraculously came simultaneously; the time was particularly auspicious, the full moon of *Mākha*, which coincides with *Śiva-rātri*. Above all, *Mākha Pūjā* is a celebration of the Sangha and, in this sense, can be seen to compliment *Visākha Pūjā*'s celebration of the Buddha and *Āsālaha Pūjā*'s primary focus on the Dhamma. On this occasion the Buddha is reputed to have preached on the *patimokkha*. His discourse constituted, in effect, a farewell address to the assembled Sangha for he also announced that he would reach his *parinibbāna* in three months. To assure a well established Order respected and supported by the people, he encouraged the assembled *arahat*s on three topics: do no evil of any kind (*sabbapāpassa akaran*), be established in the good (*kusalassa upasampadā*), maintain a clear mind (*sacitta pariyodapan*).[16]

The *Mākha Pūjā* celebration follows much the same pattern as the other two ceremonies previously discussed. At dusk, after instructions in the significance of *Mākha Pūjā* and the traditional three-fold circumambulation around the *ceitya* led by the monks and novices, the congregation returns to the *vihāra* for a service of chanting and a sermon. The traditional chant used for this ceremony is the *Ovāda Patimokkhādi Pātha* composed in the early nineteenth century by King Rama IV (King Mongut). It is a masterfully wrought summary of Buddhist teaching covering the three categories of moral virtue (*sīla*), concentration (*samādhi*), and wisdom (*paññā*) concluding with the admonition that all composite things pass away and that the Sangha must be a body of merit (*kusala-dhamma*) through the monks' constant attention and heedfulness.[17] *Mākha Pūjā*, with its emphasis on the Sangha, brings to a close our consideration of the principal *Buddhavāsa* ceremonies associated specifically with the Buddha and events in the life of the earliest Buddhist community. Taken together they celebrate the tri-partite pillars of Buddhism, the Three Gems or the Three Refuges — Buddha, Dhamma, Sangha. As such they constitute a perfect whole to which I referred earlier as a complete ritual circle. I would liken this whole to the traditional Buddhist symbol of the wheel with the axis representing the Buddha, the perimeter the Dhamma, and the spokes the Sangha. The entire structure, or if you will, the entire symbol system, depends on the Buddha. Yet, he is but a particular expression of a universal truth, the Dhamma; thus, they relate to each other as the center point to its outer perimeter. The Sangha (with a slight distortion to the metaphor!) was founded by the Buddha and held together by the Dhamma, thus relating as spokes to the axis and hub.

Throughout this section our main purpose has been to depict the Buddhist ritual/festival cycle as a celebration of the life and teaching of the Buddha through remembrance/reenactment of episodes in his life and the life of the early Buddhist community. We have also mentioned the particular importance of the model of Vessantara, the last of the canonical Jātakas, both in relationship to ordination and as an integral ingredient of *vihāra* instruction. The last ceremony to be discussed in the Buddhist orientation of Wat events directly involves Vessantara. It is the recitation of the *Vessantara Jātaka* known in Thai as *Thet Mahāchat*.

Tambiah's study of Buddhism in northeast Thailand observes that the *Thet Mahāchat* (known as the *Bun Phraawes* in northeastern Thailand) is a harvest celebration occurring in February or March and was the major festival in the village of Baan Phraan Muan where he did his field research.[18] In the Lamphun-Chiang Mai area the *Thet Mahāchat* is celebrated in the twelfth lunar month (October or November) but in recent years has declined in popularity to the extent that it can be heard only in more traditional *wats* like Wat Haripuñjaya. Tambiah's analysis divides the festival into three closely integrated parts: one related to the guardian *nāga* of the village associated with protection and ensuring rains for the next planting season; a second related to the *devas* who function as mediators between men and the gods; and the third and central part related to the recitation of the entire *Vessantara Jātaka* and the merit it accrues.[19] Even though the *Thet Mahāchat* falls at a different season in the Lamphun-Chiang Mai area than in the northeast, the structure of the ceremony is roughly the same; however, the segments are less well integrated and that part of the celebration which might be labelled Brahmanical has come to dominate the occasion. Consequently, in the Lamphun-Chiang Mai area the twelfth lunar month is identified with *Loi Kratong* or the festival of floating lights variously interpreted as propitiating the *nāga*, Hindu deities, the Buddha's footprint in the Mamatānatī River, and spirits of the deceased, rather than *Thet Mahāchat*.[20] Our analysis will not undertake the very interesting problem as to how this shift occurred. Rather, we shall examine the *Thet Mahāchat* as a model of *dāna* and *puñña* (*pun*) or self-sacrificial giving and merit, the two moral qualities most central to the ideology of popular Buddhism.

None of the Jātaka tales, whether canonical or non-canonical, is as famous throughout the Theravāda Buddhist world as Vessantara. Being so well known and readily available in English translation, I am somewhat apologetic for including a brief description of its contents here; however, it is appropriate at this point in order to clarify references to the story in Chapters I and II. The ceremonial aspects need not occupy us here. As Tambiah observes, its recitation is primarily a merit-making festival with particular sponsors providing each reader of the thirteen sections or chapters (*kan*) with money and a variety of gifts. Phya Anuman's description fits the most elaborate *Thet Mahāchat* celebration I have witnessed in the Lamphun-Chiang Mai area.[21] The occasion at Wat Haripuñjaya was somewhat more modest although it did include a reading of all thirteen sections beginning early in the morning of the full-moon sabbath day and continuing on until nearly midnight.

Vessantara was the son of Sanjaya, King of Sivi, and the last birth of the Buddha before his final appearance as Siddhattha. He married Maddī at the age of sixteen and they had two children. Now it happened that a great drought was imperiling Kāliṅga and a group of Brahmins approached Vessantara begging for his magical white elephant, Paccaya, which had rain-making powers. He willingly granted their request, thereby causing a great outcry against him on the part of the populace who prevailed upon the king to have Vessantara banished. Before his departure the prince held an almsgiving, the "Gift of the Seven Hundreds" in which he gave away most of his possessions.

Vessantara, his wife and children were then conveyed out of the city on a magnificent carriage drawn by four horses. Outside of the city four Brahmins requested his horses and then later on another asked for his chariot. These he gladly gave up and the family proceeded on foot. Finally, after a long and hard journey they came to their appointed destination, the Vaṅkagiri forest where they took up residence in two hermitages made for them by Vissakamma.

There they lived happily for four months being abundantly supplied with forest foods. At that time they were visited by an old Brahmin, Jūjaka, (Chuchok, the most popular of the thirteen sections of the *Thet Mahāchat*), whose young wife had commanded him to secure Vessantara's children as servants. Vessantara arranged to have Maddī gathering food in the forest so he could give up the children, not an easy task from a human point of view but necessary to realize more fully the quality of *dāna* or self-sacrifice. At this point in the story Sakka (i.e., Indra), assumed the form of a Brahmin and appeared before Vessantara to ask for Maddī. Vessantara consents only to have Sakka thereupon reveal his true identity and grant the prince eight boons. The boons he chose convey the gist of the ethical and teleological teachings of the Jātaka, namely, that: "he be able to return to his father's city, he condemn no man to death, he be helpful to all people, he not ever be guilty of adultery, his son should have a long life, he partake of celestial food, his ability to perform *dāna* never be diminished, he be reborn in heaven."[22] In addition to these boons everything Vessantara had sacrificed was received back again and the prince became the King of Sivi.[23]

As this brief presentation of the Jātaka tale illustrates, even though the perfection (*pāramitā*) of self-sacrificial giving is being lifted up here, the ending gives a very different twist to that virtue by comparison to the model of Siddhattha's renunciation. The audience listens to those episodes in the *Thet Mahāchat* where Vessantara and his family endure the hardships of their journey or the pathos of giving up one's beloved children knowing that in the end the prince will get in return more than he has given up, including a heavenly rebirth. As a heroic legend filled with teachings of a popular morality, colorful characters like Jūjaka, and a reward of prosperity and guarantee of a heavenly future, the *Vessantara Jātaka* embodies the virtue of *puñña* or merit more than *dāna*. In short, the *Vessantara Jātaka* teaches the lesson of the reciprocal qualities of giving and merit which lie at the very foundation of Buddhist morality. Furthermore, the reciprocal mechanism of giving and merit is the principal justification for most *Buddhavāsa* ceremonies (*phitī kamma*).

The Cosmic-Natural Orientation

In Chapters I and II we claimed that the founding of the Haripuñjaya kingdom and the structure of the Wat displayed cosmic symbolism. The *r̥si* Vasudeva of Mt. Sutep looking in all directions and establishing a town with a populace whose lineage stemmed from four locations, and the *ceitya/vihāra* plan of the Wat were used among other examples to illustrate this claim. On the festival level as well, a similar orientation may be substantiated both in terms of specific Wat festivals as well as sub-themes of ceremonies whose primary interpretative ideology is Buddhist. Tambiah's analysis of the cycle of collective *wat* rites illustrates how the entire ritual/festival year is, indeed, geared into the cycle of nature or the agricultural cycle.[24] In short, the ritual/festival cycle of the Wat reflects a Buddhist or moral-ontological calendar and a cosmic-natural calendar which are more or less intertwined. While all events in the cycle bear at least a secondary Buddhist interpretation, some take a primary bearing from the natural cycle.

In the light of the preponderance of the Buddhist orientation on the cognitive level in the ritual/festival cycle of the Wat, this section and the following one will be more limited in scope than the preceding one. Here our focus will be on the celebration of the Thai New Year (*songkrān*), a rich and varied festival covering a period of from three to five days. As in the preceding analysis, the present discussion aims to facilitate the general proposal of this study rather than merely being comprehensive. In this case our focus is the way in which *songkrān* symbolizes the renewal of sacred time.

Northern Thailand celebrates Thai New Year more energetically and more extensively than any other part of the country. Natives of Chiang Mai observe somewhat cynically that the festival has all but been taken over by the Thailand Tourist Organization and its deeper, religious significance lost in the deluge of Bangkok tourists who flood the city at this time. Lamphun, fortunately, has been spared somewhat from the corroding effects of the tourist and the celebration there is both more modest and its structure more visible.

Songkrān (from the Sanskrit, *saṅkrānti*) means to "move to another place" and refers to the time when, according to Brahmanical reckoning, the sun leaves the sign of Pisces in the zodiac and enters that of Aries. Usually, this passage falls on April 13 with the *songkrān* festival lasting through the 15th, 16th or 17th depending on the location. Coming as it does at the end of the dry season (approximately October through April), the traditional Thai New Year is fraught with sympathetic magic gauged to bring forth the rains in anticipation of the rice planting season, and the more profound symbolism of new beginnings. As a New Year celebration incorporated into the Wat ritual/festival cycle, only the Wat Haripuñjaya annual anniversary celebration surpasses it in sheer size and popularity.

Songkrān, a Brahmanical ceremony from South India, was probably adapted to Buddhism in Śri Lanka.[25] The Thai texts describing the origin of the New Year festival were originally Sinhalese and were probably brought to Thailand by a Thai monk during the Sukhothai period. The etiological myth of its origin related below is certainly Brahmanical.

> Once there was a wealthy couple who had no children. Their home was near the dwelling of a drunken n'er-do-well who had two children with golden colored skin. One day the n'er-do-well in a drunken rage berated his wealthy neighbors by shouting that the most defaming thing to someone with wealth was not to have children to inherit that wealth. The couple felt very sorrowful and prayed to the *devata* for three years that they might have a child. Finally, at the time of *songkrān* they took an offering of rice and having washed it seven times presented it to a large banyan tree growing on the river bank and prayed for a son. The tree *devata* was moved by compassion and pleaded their

cause to Indra that they might have a son. Indra in turn granted them their wish. The wealthy couple named the boy Dhammapāla and built a seven storied palace for him near the banyan tree. The boy was especially clever. He learned the language of birds and memorized the three Vedas by the time he was seven. He was especially adept as a fortune-teller.

At that time everyone in the world worshipped the Lord Mahā-Brahma, and Kapila-Brahma who had the power to cast fortune on all men. When Kapila-Brahma heard about Dhammapāla he went to see him and proposed a wager: that he would ask three questions and if Dhammapāla was unable to answer within seven days he would be beheaded but if he answered them correctly then the same fate would be in store for Kapila-Brahama. The three questions were: Where is the zodiac (*rāsi*) in the morning, in the afternoon, and in the evening?

Six days passed and Dhammapāla still had not discovered the answer. Knowing he would be killed the next day according to the terms of the wager he decided it would be better to hide and simply starve to death; so, he descended from his palace and found his way to two palm trees beneath which he fell asleep. Two eagles were in the palm trees and at dusk the female asked her mate what they would eat the next day. The mate replied that they would eat the body of Dhammapāla who would be killed by Kapila-Brahma since the boy could not answer the three questions. The female asked what the questions were and when her mate replied she asked how they should be answered. Her mate answered, 'In the morning the zodiac is at our face so we wash our face; in the afternoon it is at our breast so we sprinkle the breast with scented water; in the evening it is at our feet so we wash our feet.'

Dhammapāla, hearing this, returned to the palace. The next day when the Lord Kapila-Brahma came the boy was able to answer the questions. Kapila-Brahma sent for the seven *devata* of Indra. 'I must cut off my head as an offering for Dhammapāla,' he said. 'However, if my head is put in the earth, the earth will be consumed in fire; if cast into the air there will be no more rain; if put in the ocean it will be dried up. Therefore, let these seven *devata* take my head around Mt. Sumeru within sixty minutes time and then put it in the cave in Mt. Kailasa made out of seven precious stones by Visvakamma and made into a meeting room for the *devata* by Lakshmi. The *devata* should then make propitiatory offerings for 365 days which constitutes one year. Then, at *songkrān*, the seven *devata* of Indra should take my head around Mt. Sumeru again.'[26]

The first day of *songkrān*, known in Thai as *wan sang khān long*, signifies the end of the old year. Houses are thoroughly cleansed, trash burned, clothes and hair washed. Firecrackers can be heard exploding from midnight onwards until dawn. In short, the first day of the New Year festival aims at banishing the accumulated demerits of the past year. The second day of the festival (*wan naw*) serves as a day of preparation for the following day, usually the most significant Wat celebration. Special foods and sweetmeats are prepared to be taken to the Wat the next morning as food offerings to the monks. In the late afternoon and early evening sand from the nearby Mae Kuang River is brought in buckets by hundreds of people to be piled into an enormous sand *ceitya*. The third day (*wan phanāwan*) of the *songkrān* festival dawns as the first day of the New Year and, hence, is traditionally considered the most auspicious day of the year. For this reason ordinations, house dedications and other particularly auspicious (*monkhon*) occasions may be held on this day.[27] At Wat Haripuñjaya crowds of people come bearing food as a meritorious offering to the monks for their morning meal. Following the presentation of food, monks, novices and laity gather in the main *vihāra* for a service of chanting and a sermon, usually a traditional New Year sermon (*anisong pī mai*) appropriate to the merit-making potential of this occasion. The sand *ceitya* will have been completed and is presented (*dāna*) at this service. It is topped by three flags or banners variously interpreted as symbolizing the Buddha, Dhamma, Sangha or, together with the *ceitya* itself, said to represent the two major components of sentient existence, name (*nāma*) and form (*rūpa*). A white cord (*sai sin*) stretches from the main Buddha image in the *vihāra* to the sand *ceitya*.

The sand *ceitya* functions as the focal point of the cosmic-natural significance of the Thai New Year festival. It points to new beginnings both on the macro-cosmic as well as the micro-cosmic levels. Charged with power from the Buddha image through the conduit provided by the *sai sin*,[28] it symbolizes the regeneration of the individual (*nāma/rūpa*) and the reordering of the world. This structural meaning of the sand *ceitya* which, in effect, encapsulates the cosmic-natural level of meaning of the entire New Year celebration, reflects the anticipated arrival of the monsoon rains and the planting of paddy rice. The meaning of new beginnings is even latent in one of the practical interpretations given to the bringing of sand into the Wat compound; namely, that it re-furbishes, levels and raises the grounds. The Buddhist interpretation of the origin of the *ceitya*, at least as local lore has it, is as follows: In a previous existence the Buddha was a poor man who made his living gathering firewood. Even though he was poor he was very virtuous. One day while walking in the forest in search of dead tree limbs he came across a place covered with clean sand. There he built a sand *ceitya*, put a small flag made from a torn piece of cloth on top of it, and then prayed that he might be reborn a Buddha for the benefit of all sentient beings.[29]

The events of the remainder of the third day of *songkrān* and the fourth day differ from town to town and from *wat* to *wat*. At Wat Haripuñjaya afternoon activities are informal. Lay people may wander in to pay their respects to the Buddha image, to visit respected monks, or to purchase fish or small caged birds to free. This practice of freeing fish and birds in order to gain merit may be done at any time but is particularly associated with the Thai New Year festival. The following Buddhist legend recounts the origin of this practice. Sāriputra once had a novice disciple by the name of Sukha. One day in a vision Sāriputra sees that his disciple will die that very evening. Sukha requests permission to return to his home and on the way notices a fish which has been cast up out of the water on the bank. Carefully he puts the fish back in the water thereby saving its life. When he reaches home he informs his parents of his immanent death. Grief-stricken, they prepare him in burial clothes, light incense, and settle into a final vigil over their son. Miraculously, however, in the morning he is still alive. Surprised and overjoyed beyond words, Sukha returns to his teacher, Sāriputra, relates the episode of his journey home, and his miraculous recovery. Sāriputra explains that through the merit Sukha had gained by saving the life of the fish his own life was prolonged.[30] The freeing of fish and birds and other animals on particularly auspicious occasions may be interpreted in terms of the above legend as building up sufficient merit to prolong one's life, or in a more ethical sense as helping a person to be filled with loving-kindness (*metta/karuṇā*) toward all living beings in the world.[31]

The fourth day of *sonkrān* (*wan pāk pī*) at Wat Haripuñjaya centers on paying respects to the leading monks of the Wat, in particular the abbot who is also the head of the northern region. Monks and lay men and women from all over the town come throughout the day. As on the preceding day, in the morning food offerings are presented to the monks and a preaching service is held. Holy water (*nam som poy*), charged with sacred power by chanting, is poured over the hands of the abbot by lay leaders of the Wat. It is also used to annoint the *ceitya* and Buddha images in a form of ritual cleansing and purification. Here again the theme of new beginnings is apparent. Just as the first day of the New Year's festival is devoted to the actual cleansing of homes, the third and fourth days include the ritual cleansing of sacred objects at the Wat. Similarly, paying respects (*tam hua*) to high ranking monks and respected lay persons on the third, fourth and last day (*wan pāk du'an*) of *songkrān* symbolizes the seeking of forgiveness, wiping the slate clean for the beginning of the New Year. In this connection we might note that traditionally debts were settled (not necessarily paid in full) at this time. While it is not the case at Wat Haripuñjaya, at some *wat*s the main ceremony of paying respects to monks, elders, and sacred *wat* objects takes place on the third day of the New Year festivities and the focus of the fourth day is a Brahmanical ceremony for dispelling misfortune (*song khrq*) conducted at the *wat* but led by a layman and not by one of the monks.[32] Throughout the New Year festival the juxtaposition of Buddhist and Brahmanical elements is particularly interesting but outside of the focus of the main interpretative thrust of this study.

One omni-present element of the *songkrān* festival has not yet been mentioned — water throwing. In the north throughout the three or four day celebration young people delight in throwing water on unwary passersby. Oftentimes this water-throwing gets completely out of hand, especially in Chiang Mai, where the governor usually calls for more decorous behavior than the previous year. This part of the festival, on the one hand, provides pure entertainment for young people. Yet, at a more profound level this kind of rowdy, even gross behavior, not to be tolerated at other times during the year, celebrates the casting away of the old and the engendering of the new.

We have mentioned the fact that Tambiah coordinates the cycle of *wat* rites with the agricultural calendar. Several aspects of ritual/festival events at Wat Haripuñjaya reflect their connection with the cosmic cycle of the movement of nature; however, none more clearly than *songkrān*. Here passage from old to new is clearly rooted in the seasonal change, anticipation of the monsoon rains, and the planting of new crops. The day by day events, each in their own particular way, highlight the several facets of annual renewal, e.g., cleansing, forgiving, paying respects, the sand *ceitya*, etc., nor can the Buddhist interpretations belie the fact that the primary orientation of *songkrān* stems from much more archaic roots.

The Socio-Political Orientation

We have demonstrated the overlap between the Buddhist and socio-political orders in the chronicle accounts. In particular we argued that King Ādittarāja, as the Buddha's counterpart, actualizes the Buddha's power thereby establishing order in the socio-political realm. It was suggested, furthermore, that this same overlap is evidenced in the Wat structure simply in the connection between the symbolism of the relic and the *cakkavattin* (universal monarch). This section will demonstrate how that relationship is enacted in the annual festival of Wat Haripuñjaya, and to a lesser extent in the celebration of *Āsālaha Pūjā*.

Every major *wat* in northern Thailand customarily has an annual festival. Often they are held in conjunction with another event as is the case, for example, at Wat Cedī Luang in the nearby city of Chiang Mai where the annual festival falls at the same time as the celebration in honor of the principal guardian spirit of the city whose shrine resides in the Wat compound. While I have not made an extensive study of annual *wat* festivals, the ones I have observed with some care have taken place in the month of May at the beginning of the rainy season and, consequently, include rain-provoking, magical activities. For example, the principle Buddha image in the procession held during the Wat Cedī Luang annual festival is reputed to have rain-making powers. It should also be noted that of all the events in the ritual/festival cycles of northern Thai *wats* none exceeds these for pure entertainment value. Indeed, they are often referred to simply as *wat* fairs and include numerous vendors of food and trinkets, carnival booths, films, northern Thai dancing, competing loudspeakers on high volume, and an occasion for shy — and some not so shy — heterosexual contact on the part of young teenagers.

The climax and conclusion of the Wat Haripuñjaya annual festival falls on the full-moon sabbath during the month of May which usually coincides with *Visākha Pūjā*. This day is preceded by a week of festivities which remind the Western observer of old-fashioned carnivals. The Wat school grounds are filled with the stalls of vendors of various kinds, games of chance, and numerous amusements. Such entertainment, as mentioned above, is typical of the annual festivals (*ngan prajam pī*) of other important *wats*, especially those with a district (*tambon*) status. The following discussion is concerned only with the events of the last day itself.

The celebration begins early in the morning at approximately 7:00 A.M. with the traditional presentation of food to the monks (*tak pāt*). On this occasion, however, the number of laymen and women present exceeds any other auspicious occasion. They form a double line from the entrance of the *vihāra* along the extent of its side and reaching beyond the *ceitya*. After the food presentation and throughout the day during the 1973 celebration some of the senior monks and members of the management committee (*kammakan wat*) were seated in one of the Wat's open pavillions collecting money to purchase a set of Buddha images correlated with the days of the week (*phra prajam wan*). These images function somewhat as personal guardian deities, the particular image corresponding with one's birthday to be honored on that day. This custom was adopted in northern Thailand during the Burmese period although it is not widely practiced today. Rangoon's Swedegon Pagoda provides a good example of the *phra prajam wan* where they form a prominent adjunct to the perimeter of the base of the pagoda and offerings before these images are made more or less continuously.[33]

The largest portion of the morning is devoted to a hot-air balloon competition (*khom loi*). *Wat*s from all over Lamphun Province enter the competition contributing large tissue paper balloons from which strings of firecrackers are suspended. As the air inside the balloon is heated by inserting a bamboo pole with ignited kerosene rags on the end, it is not unusual to see one occasionally go up in flames. Once the balloon is ready, having been prepared by both the young lay men and novices of the Wat, the fuse to the long string of firecrackers is lit. Then, amidst cheers of encouragement by loyal supporters, the balloon is released to soar (hopefully!) high into the sky, fireworks blazing.

Several explanations of the meaning of *khom loi* are offered. Most informants who simply enjoy participating in or watching the competition see it as bringing a modest degree of honor to those *wat*s whose balloons perform the best. A more religiously sophisticated but not totally dissimilar explanation sees the flight of the balloon as a sign of merit with the balloon soaring the highest earning the most merit for those who made it. A third interpretation puts the *khom loi* in the same category as the rocket festival in northeastern Thailand which, as Tambiah argues, is basically related to rain-making.[34] Indeed, another May *wat* festival I witnessed in the Lamphun countryside included both a balloon and a rocket competition. A fourth interpretation according to one informant is a mythic account in an old northern chronicle (*tamnān*) where it is recorded that the balloons convey offerings to the Culāmanī *ceitya* in Tāvatimsa heaven established there by Sakka (Indra) to enshrine the Buddha's top-knot and jewelled turban thrown into the sky at the time of his renunciation.[35] In turn, Sakka showers blessings (rain?) on those who send offerings to the Culāmanī.

Following the balloon competition in the early afternoon the long drum (*klong luang*) competition commences. The northern Thai long drum is a very distinctive instrument. The base, consisting of a hollowed piece of teak measuring from ten to fifteen feet in length and mounted on wheels, gives a profound and haunting resonance. Traditionally the long drum would be sounded at intervals the evening prior to the Buddhist sabbath, its subdued and mournful tones reverberating across the countryside. Only a few *wats* continue to observe this custom even though most of them still own at least one drum. For the competition at the Wat Haripuñjaya festival *wats* from all over Lamphun brought their long drums into the Wat compound to see which would be judged to have the best tone and be beaten the most skillfully. During the competition the drum is struck very rapidly until the drummer's arm is exhausted. A piece of cloth is wound around the drummer's hand making a cone shape. Even so, the pressure exerted during the drumming has been known to break a wrist or a hand.

The drum competition, as with the balloon competition, is liable to several interpretations. Most informants see it merely as part of the entertainment of the festival. Its most probable significance ties into the ideology of merit and reward. One northern Thai text, the *Tamnān Daw Duang*, offers the following particularly picturesque explanation. Once upon a time one of the *yakkha*s (demons) decided that mankind should be destroyed because all men are so evil. Indra, hearing of the *yakkha*'s intentions pleads with the demon on the behalf of mankind. Indra is getting nowhere with his arguments until, in the midst of his intercession, the sound of long drum is heard being struck before the Buddhist sabbath. Indra then succeeds in convincing the *yakkha* that all men must not be evil or they would not be hearing the sound of the long drum announcing the Buddha *pūjā*. Indra, thereby, saves or rewards those who perform meritorious deeds, in this case, the beating of the long drum.

The focal point of the day's celebration, the annointing of the *ceitya*-reliquary, takes place in the mid-afternoon. This part of the festival dramatizes the close relationship that pertains between the religious and the socio-political realms. It actually began the preceding day when water was brought to the Lamphun provincial government office from a seemingly insignificant well on Mt. Kha Mọ outside of Lamphun. The well and the water from it are considered sacred for they figure into the mythic-legend of the Buddha's visit to northern Thailand (see Chapter 1). Several *wats* in the Lamphun area are associated with the events of that visit designating, for example, where the Buddha slept, where he washed and dried his robes, and where he ate. One of these holy sites is associated with the miraculous appearance of a spring to quench the Buddha's thirst after he ate. According to the legend, finding no water in the immediate vicinity, the Buddha pressed his thumb to the ground and a spring immediately appeared there. Tradition has it that the spring always has water and that it is never brackish. Women are forbidden to touch the water and if they do it must be purified by appropriate chants (*suat mantra*).[36]

On the morning of the full-moon sabbath, sacred water (*nam phra rāja dāna*) blessed by the King of Thailand is sent from Bangkok to the provincial office. In the mid-afternoon it is placed in a palanquin and brought in a procession of government officials, boy scouts, and school children along with the water from Mt. Kha Mǫ, into the Wat compound now crowded once again with people. First the water sent by the King makes its way by pulley up the *ceitya* where it is used to lustrate the dome, followed by the water taken from the sacred spring. Then senior government officials and civil servants who had been in the procession annoint the *ceitya*. Afterwards the people who came to witness the event throw their own lustral water on the sacred monument. After the *ceitya*-reliquary has been duly sanctified by lustral water from the King, the sacred well, and the government personnel, it is then draped with a new saffron cloth also sent by the King.

The remainder of the afternoon is filled with processions from various Lamphun *wat*s to Wat Haripuñjaya. These include home-made floats, bands, and girls performing northern Thai dances. By late afternoon and early evening delegations from all of the districts of Lamphun Province will have gathered at the Wat in preparation for the evening's activities. These include circumambulating the *ceitya*, listening to sermons and chanting (*suat berk*) in all four of the *vihāra*. Each of the districts is assigned to a particular *vihāra* and the monks of that district are responsible for the service held there. The services continue through the night. Traditional sermons preached include the Buddha's first discourse, the account of Prince Siddhattha's renunciation, and a sermon covering the major episodes of the Buddha's life recited in conjunction with the discussion of *Visākha Pūjā*. The chanting for this occasion, *suat berk*, is a special northern Thai style used almost exclusively for consecrations. The festival is brought to a close the next morning when once again food is presented to the monks.

The culminating day of the Wat Haripuñjaya annual festival, which centers on the annointing of the *ceitya*-reliquary (*song nam phradhātu*), combines three elements. First, it is a festival of national integration symbolized in particular by the lustral water sent by the King, and also by the participation by government leaders on the provincial and district levels. Second, it is a festival of social and religious integration. All ecclesiastical district heads are in attendance as well as representatives from all of the major *wat*s in the province. Also note that the ceremonies lasting through the night take place in all four *vihāra* surrounding the *ceitya*, the only time during the year when this occurs. Third, it is a festival of renewal, symbolizing — as in the case of *Visākha Pūjā* and *songkrān* — both an end and a new beginning.

In addition to the *ngan song nām phradhātu*, the King's special relationship to Wat Haripuñjaya as one of the 147 royal *wat*s throughout the country, is affirmed during the *Āsālaha Pūjā* celebration at the beginning of the Rains Retreat. On this occasion the King sends a large candle presumed sufficient to burn through the period of *vassā*. Once again the reciprocal relationship between the political and religious orders is symbolized in the procession of the King's *vassā* candle from the headquarters of the provincial government to the Wat. As is the case at the Wat's annual festival provincial and district government officials participate and one of the chief officers of Lamphun Province leads in a brief dedicatory service held in the main *vihāra*. The relationship between the religious and political orders, as suggested above, is reciprocal or symbiotic. For example, the annointing of the *ceitya*-reliquary with the holy water blessed by the King in one sense symbolizes the honor and respect paid to Buddhism by the state. On the other hand, however, in the ritual cleansing of the sacred monument the symbol of the King's presence (i.e., the royal lustral water) takes precedence over the water taken from the sacred well associated with the Buddha. In short, I am suggesting that the heart of Wat Haripuñjaya's annual festival is a reenactment of the mutual inter-dependence of the religious and socio-political orders.

The Wat as a religious center provides the arena for the ritual and festival reenactment of a sacred time measured in terms of a sacred history calculated according to the events in the biography of the founder, and a sacred time measured through recurring, seasonal change. Furthermore, the power of the King and by extension his duly appointed government officers, sanctifies and reenforces both interrelated calendars through symbolic and actual participation in selected strategic events. Thus, while we legitimately distinguish differing "orientations" in the ritual/festival cycle of Wat Haripuñjaya, we wish to conclude this chapter by reiterating that these distinctive elements cannot belie the inherent unity to be found in the celebratory life of the Wat.

[1]See H. K. Kaufman, *Bangkhuad, A Community Study in Thailand* (New York: J. J. Augustus, Inc., 1960) for a thorough discussion of the varied functions of the village *wat*.

[2]Frank E. Reynolds makes a similar point in his *Buddhism and Sacred Kingship* . . . . See also S. J. Tambiah, *Buddhism and the Spirit Cults* . . . , pp. 337ff.

[3]While Melford Spiro emphasizes the differences between Nibbanic and Kammatic Buddhism he also points out their inter-relationships. See Melford E. Spiro, *Buddhism and Society: A Great Tradition and Its Burmese Vicissitudes* (New York: Harper & Row, 1970).

[4]One informant at a novitiate ordination claimed that the princely dress worn by the young boys in the ceremony could be interpreted as either Vessantara or Siddhattha. In my own opinion the juxtaposition of the Vessantara and Siddhattha motifs can help put such events as the ordination ceremony into a context which serves to enhance our understanding of the meaning of the tradiion.

[5]Sukumar Dutt, *Early Buddhist Monarchism* (Bombay: Asia Publishing House, 1960), chaps. III & IV.

[6]*Ibid.*, chap. V.

[7]This point raises the problem of the vicious circle inherent in merit-making activities; namely, that the rich can afford elaborate merit-making and, thereby, accrue more merit. The poor, for the

same reason, have less opportunity to earn merit. While normative Buddhism emphasizes the intention of the deed as much or more than the result, in actual practice most informants indicate their belief that the quantitatively larger gift accrues more merit. There seems to be little of the "it is harder for the rich man to enter the Kingdom of Heaven than the camel to go through the eye of a needle" mentality when it comes to the mechanism of merit-making.

[8]Adapted from Kenneth E. Wells, *Thai Buddhism* . . . , pp. 164-65. See also Plaek Santhiraksa, *Latthi Prapenī lae Phithī Kamma* (Bangkok: Pannākhān, 1972), pp. 302 ff.; Sanguan Chotisakkaratana, *Prapenī Lānnā Thai lae Phithī Kamma Tang Tang* (Chiang Mai: Prathu'ang Withayā, 1973), pp. 159-60.

[9]Plaek Santhiraksa, *op. cit.*, p. 130.

[10]*Ibid.*, p. 274.

[11]Nāng Thoranī, a feminine deity personifying the creative forces of the earth is a very popular mythic figure in Thai Buddhism. She appears frequently in temple wall paintings representing the episode from the Buddha's life referred to in the text. Statues of Nāng Thoranī wringing water from her hair are a relatively familiar sight in Thai *wat* compounds. One stands on the perimeter of the Wat Haripuñjaya ceitya and lay persons frequently make offerings before it.

[12]Plaek Santhiraksa, *op. cit.*, pp. 135-62.

[13]*Ibid.*, pp. 167-68. Also, Sanguan Chotisakkaratana, *Prapenī Lānnā Thai* . . . , pp. 160-61.

[14]Plaek Santhiraksa, *op. cit.*, p. 299.

[15]Richard Gombrich, *Precept and Practice* . . . , p. 4.

[16]Plaek Santhiraksa, *op. cit.*, p. 241.

[17]See translation in Kenneth E. Wells, *Thai Buddhism* . . . , pp. 80-84, taken from the Royal Book of Chants.

[18]S. J. Tambiah, *Buddhism and the Spirit Cults* . . . , pp. 160-61.

[19]*Ibid.*, pp. 161-68.

[20]Kenneth E. Wells, *Thai Buddhism* . . . , pp. 111-14; Sanguan Chotisakkaratana, *Prapenī Thai Phāk Nu'a* (Chiang Mai: Sapha-dhamma-vijaya, 1968), pp. 55-66.

[21]Phya Anuman Rajadhon, *Essays on Thai Folklore* (Bangkok: Social Science Association Press, 1968), pp. 36-48.

[22]G. P. Malalasekere, *Dictionary of Pāli Proper Names*, vol. 2 (London: Luzac & Co., 1967), p. 946.

[23]See Phya Anuman Rajadhon, *Essays on Thai Folklore*, pp. 164-77; S. J. Tambiah, *Buddhism and the Spirit Cults* . . . , pp. 160ff.

[24]S. J. Tambiah, *op. cit.*, chap. X.

[25]Plaek Santhiraksa, *op. cit.*, p. 253.

[26]*Ibid.*, pp. 259-63.

[27]Sanguan Chotisakkarantana, *Prapenī Thai Phāk Nu'a* (Bangkok: Odian, 1972), p. 6.

[28]The *sai sin* or *sai sincana* is a white cord made up of three separate strands often interpreted as symbolizing the Three Gems. It is a necessary element of every merit-making ceremony where chanting occurs. It extends from the Buddha image through the hands of the monks who are chanting. If the ceremony focuses on a particular object such as a casket containing the deceased at a funeral, then the *sai sin* will be tied to that object. The cord functions as a conduit of power conveying it from its source (the Buddha) having been released by the mechanism of the chant.

[29]Sanguan Chotisakkaratana, *Prapenī Thai Phāk Nu'a* (1972), pp. 13-14.

[30]*Ibid.*, pp. 15-16.

[31]*Ibid.*, p. 17.

[32]For a discussion of *songkrān* see Sanguan Chotisakkarantana, *Prapenī Thai Phāk Nu'a* (2509), pp. 119-27.

[33]See Shway Yoe, *The Burman: His Life and Notions* (New York: Norton & Co., 1963), chap. XV, for a description of the Swedegon Pagoda.

[34]S. J. Tambiah, *op. cit.*, p. 286.

[35]Henry Warren, *Buddhism in Translations* (Cambridge: Harvard Unversity Press, 1947), p. 66.

[36]Here is another taboo to counter the power of women. We saw an earlier example in the taboo prohibiting women from entering the compound of the Wat Haripuñjaya *ceitya*.

Chapter IV

The Wat as an Educational Center

In the previous three chapters the thrust of this study has been to look for the inter-relationships between the moral-ontological, cosmic-natural, and socio-political orders within the varying symbol systems of Wat Haripuñjaya: historical chronicles, the physical structures of the Wat, and the ritual/festival cycles. In this and the next chapter we shall see how the Wat functions practically as an educational and administrative center. In both cases, our contention will be that the Wat or the religious realm (*sāsanacakra*) parallels the secular realm or the socio-political order (*ānācakra*). Metaphorically, these 'two wheels of Dhamma' might be depicted as moving on the same axis, each supporting the other; thus, the parallelism implies various kinds of inter-dependence and interaction.[1] In particular, religious education provides the moral basis for Thai citizenship or identity, a symbiosis which may become more tenuous in the face of recent unprecedented political events.[2] This chapter will first describe the educational scene at Wat Haripuñjaya and then proceed with a discussion of the content of religious instruction with the aim of showing that Buddhist studies (*dhamma-su'ksā*) at the Wat boys' school serve to reinforce the moral-ethical basis of the socio-political order and that Pāli studies sanctify and perpetuate the religious order in particular. Some attention will be given to the apparent tension between the ethos established by the traditional Buddhist studies curriculum and recent political events, and the potential implications of this tension for the Sangha. Furthermore, it will be pointed out that the problem raised offers a new perspective on the interpretative model on which this study rests, an issue to be addressed again in our conclusion.

Contrary to the view of the early Buddhist monastic community as lonely mendicants plying various methods of meditation aimed at the realization of Nibbāna, both the early Sutta material and the *Mahāvagga* depict the Sangha with the Buddha at its head as fundamentally involved in the teaching enterprise. The Buddha is primarily a teacher who instructs both monks and laity and is only incidentally a yogic miracle-worker. Furthermore, the importance of institutional Buddhism as a teaching center is reflected in the traditional division of monastic activities between study (*ganthadhura*) and meditation (*vipassanadhura*). In short, from the beginning, institutional

Buddhism has been involved in education.

In Thailand, as in other Theravāda Buddhist countries, literacy was traditionally associated with the monastery and the court, the two principle bearers of Indian culture. In the monastery, education in Buddhist doctrine and history, Pāli, the Thai language, and such specialized subjects as astrology and traditional medicine was conducted in an informal manner (viz., by way of contrast to a modern school situation). From the evidence of extant *wat* libraries in the north we can infer that particular abbots took a special interest in education, probably attracting some of the most able monks and novices as students. This situation prevailed until the middle of the 19th century when, during the reign of Rama IV and with the help of missionaries from the West, private schools outside the *wat* were established. From the time of the establishment of the first public schools to the present, secular schools have increasingly dominated Thai education. Special religious instruction is now either conducted separately as part of monastic training or, on the level of the laity, is one part of the required curriculum. Today Thai primary and secondary education is carefully controlled by the Ministry of Education which prescribes the curriculum and sets the final examination standards students must meet for entrance to the university. The schools at Wat Haripuñjaya form but one small piece of this educational picture; however, not an insignificant one either in Lamphun Province or for the Sangha on a nation-wide basis. In order to get an idea of the overall educational situation in Lamphun the following chart indicates the number of secular schools and centers of Buddhist and Pāli studies in the entire province.[3]

Name of District	Provincial Schools	District Schools	Private Schools	Municipal Schools	Religious Studies	
					Buddhism	Pali
Lamphun	4	86	4	4	21	4
Pāsāng	1	60	1	—	14	1
Ban Hong	1	37	1	—	6	1
Lī	1	55	—	—	6	—
Mae Thā	—	34	—	—	2	—
Total	7	273	6	4	49	6

Education at Wat Haripuñjaya can be roughly divided into religious and secular education. The largest school is the boys' school begun by the present abbot and manager (*phu jat kān*) in 2489 B.E. (1946 A.D.). Its 1974 enrollment totalled 1310 including 493 novices and 37 monks in eight grades, the final three of seven primary (*prathom*) grades, and the five secondary grades (*mathyom*).[4] Forty-six teachers of whom twenty-four are monks teach the graduated curriculum covering social studies, Thai, English, science, math, gym, and boy scouts. An additonal fifteen monks offer instruction in Buddhist studies and Pāli. The school day runs from eight in the morning to three in the afternoon for the lay children while the monks and novices at the school have three hours of Buddhist studies and Pāli from two to five in the afternoon. The school has an annual operating budget of approximately 400,000 baht (approximately $20,000) of which over half is exhausted by salaries ranging from $12 to $65 per month with both monks and laymen being compensated equally for equal tenure and work. Three-fourths of the operating cost of the school is defrayed by school fees and one fourth or approximately 100,000 baht by government subsidy.

Throughout the entire country there are only fifty *wat* schools offering secular studies in the upper primary and lower secondary grades. The school at Wat Haripuñjaya is one of only two schools providing the final two years (college preparatory) of instruction. Only at Wat Haripuñjaya and in Petchaburi in south central Thailand can monks and novices receive college preparatory work. Consequently, all districts of Lamphun Province are represented at the school as well as the northern provinces of Lampang, Chiang Mai, Chiangrai, Prae, Nan and Mae Hong Son.

It was the opinion of most of my informants that the predominating role of the Wat was education. Clearly the school provides an important avenue for educational and, hence, social advancement for young novices whose families probably would not be able to afford an education for them otherwise. Fully ninety percent of the monks and novices graduating from the third secondary level (M.S. 3) leave the monastic life and either take a secular job or go on for further training elsewhere. Of those who do not leave the Order, however, many have gone on to become important ecclesiastical leaders in their own districts and provinces. As a result, over the more than twenty-five years of its existence, the boys' school at Wat Haripuñjaya has served two functions for the monks and novices it has trained: it has enabled many young men to get an education and, thereby, find a responsible job in Thai society; and, it has provided many of the leaders in the Sangha in the northern provinces. With some pride the head teacher told me that graduates of the school have a reputation for honesty and hard work, and that those who stay in the Sangha are much more scientifically minded and less superstitious than their peers who have not had the advantage of their education.

What about the religious instruction at the boys' school at Wat Haripuñjaya? Does it differ in any way from the government curriculum in ethics (*sīla-dhamma*) required through all grades of primary and secondary study? Indeed, it does and this difference received much emphasis in my interviews at the school. In the first place, the monks and novices are required to take both Buddhist studies and Pāli for three hours in the afternoon. They exemplify most clearly the parallelism between the "two wheels of Dhamma" in the educational sphere for their mornings are devoted to secular studies and their afternoons to religious studies. As to the relative importance given to the two foci the high percentage of monks and novices who leave the Order upon graduation give testimony to the primacy of secular studies. A similar observation would hold true for lay students. While they study a more demanding religious studies curriculum than students at government schools outside the Wat, few expend the same effort on Buddhist studies as they do on their secular subjects. Nevertheless, from the standpoint of material covered, time spent, and quality of instruction their exposure to Buddhist thought and practice is superior. At this point, we shall examine in some detail that portion of the curriculum especially relevant to the thrust of this chapter, namely, the moral-ethical basis that religious instruction articulates for the socio-political order.

Religious Instruction (dhamma-su'ksā)

Religious instruction or instruction in Buddhist history, doctrine, ethics and practice takes basically two forms in primary and secondary education in Thailand. Ordinarily most schools, whether government or private, follow the prescribed series of textbooks in ethics (sīla-dhamma) prepared by the Ministry of Education. Wat schools like Haripuñjaya, however, teach from the books used by monks and novices in preparing for the three-tiered exams in Buddhist studies (nāga dhamma)[5] omitting those portions relevant only to the monastic regime (i.e., Vinaya). This curriculum was established during the reign of Rama VI (1910-1925) by the most impressive Sangharāja of the modern period, Prince Vajirañāna. It is a graduated curriculum with varying titles in sequence covering the following subject areas: Buddhist doctrine, Buddhist history including the life of the Buddha and his most famous disciples, monastic discipline, and Buddhist rites and rituals. Monk, novice, or lay student graduating from the Wat Haripuñjaya boys' school has a reasonably proficient knowledge of Buddhist history and teachings and, even more important from the standpoint of the Sangha, has received instruction in the numerous Buddhist ceremonies and festivals punctuating the religious year including chants appropriate for each one. Consequently, his principal religious instruction has taken place within the context of a school, albeit the Wat school. The same observation would hold true, however, for lay students at government schools although they would receive less instruction. One approach to religious instruction in schools would be to investigate the way in which it reinforces the religious order as alluded to above. Our interest, however, is to relate it to the socio-political order. Toward this end we shall examine relevant portions of the most famous textbook of beginning Dhamma studies, the Navakovāda, and the ethical ideal of what we might characterize as the good citizen as depicted in the government ethics curriculum (sīla-dhamma).

The curriculum of both Dhamma-study (dhamma-su'ksā) and the sīla-dhamma government curriculum cover the same general subject matter areas, i.e., Buddhist history, ceremonies, doctrine and ethical teachings. The main difference lies in the greater detail of the Dhamma-study books and the fact that the students at the Wat Haripuñjaya boys' school are required to spend more time in instruction in Buddhism.[6] The general structure which appears to inform all religious/ethical studies in theThai schools can be formulated as follows:[7]

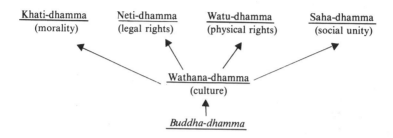

The ground of Thai culture is assumed to be Buddhism. Thus, while Thai culture gives expression to particular kinds of social behavior, the normative value of that behavior is perceived as being rooted in Buddhism. The best way to get at this proposition is to examine its two sides: relevant Buddhist ethical teachings as delineated in the curriculum; and behavior deemed appropriate to the Thai society and nation.

The ethical teachings of Theravāda Buddhism are rooted in a set of beliefs enumerated as follows: belief in the universal law of cause and effect (*hetu/phala*); the Buddha attained to the knowledge of the way of peace and equanimity; the Buddha's teaching is the truth about the nature of things and whoever is able to follow this teaching is released from ill; the Sangha is composed of persons who have a special opportunity to study the teachings of the Buddha and to try to carry them out, and is not a body primarily for the performance of rites; the world was not created by anyone and is governed only by the laws of nature; everyone has his or her own *kamma* which results in suffering (*dukkha*) or happiness (*sukha*); through special effort one overcomes the power of *kamma*; the true nature of Buddhism is not found in texts, teachings, or ceremonies but in acting according to the Truth which leads to purity, knowledge, peace and equanimity.[8] The moral and ethical teachings based on these beliefs take several traditional forms. The best known, of course, is that of the Five Precepts (*pañca-sīla*), the avoidance of taking life, stealing, illicit sex, lying, intoxicating beverages, and their positive counterparts the *pañca-dhamma*: loving kindness (*mettā-karuṇā*), right vocation (*sammā-ājīva*), sexual restraint, honesty, and a sense of right and wrong.[9] Adhering to the moral-ethical pattern advocated by these teachings produces three kinds of benefits — to oneself, to Thai society, and to the Thai nation. The individual is respected, for he chooses the good and avoids the evil; Thai society will be peaceful because its people are grounded in the Five Precepts; the nation will be happy and free from persecution because its citizens are not at enmity with one another.[10]

Another traditional formulation of Buddhist belief and practice found in the curriculum is the threefold division of: avoid doing any kind of evil (*mai tham chua*); encourage the good (*jam pen khwām dī*); clarify the mind (*tham chai hai phọng phaeo*).[11] The first two categories are divided into acts of body, speech, and mind or heart serving to delineate the Five Precepts even further. The *Navakovāda*, a textbook derived largely from the *Aṅguttara* and *Saṁyutta Nikāya* divided into groups of teachings for easy memorization, lists the following among others: 1) the four things of present value — being industrious in one's work, careful in the use of words, actions, and wealth, associating with good people, living in terms of one's income; 2) the four means of amicable association — sharing with others, talking in agreeable speech, doing things useful for others, being evenminded; 3) the five benefits of wealth — looking after one's mother and father, children and wife, servants and friends, warding off danger, sacrificial giving; 4) the six causes of ruin — drinking intoxicating liquors, wandering abroad at night, going around watching shows, gambling, having bad people as friends, being lazy.[12]

Of particular interest in the way ethical teachings are constructed in terms of a specific cosmic scheme are the so-called Six Directions taken from the *Dīgha Nikāya* (III.118): east (mother and father), south (teacher), west (wife and children), north (friends), down (servants), up (mendicants). Below are reproduced the east, the west, and the north.

East. The forward direction signifying mother and father, whom their child should uphold in five ways:

  a) they have looked after and brought up their child, so he should repay this by looking after them;
  b) he should help to look after their affairs;
  c) he should ensure the endurance of the family name;
  d) he should conduct himself in ways that make him worthy to receive the inherited wealth;
  e) when his parents have died, he should make merit and make it over to them.

His mother and father having been upheld in the above ways should then help their child in five ways:

  a) by not letting him do evil;
  b) by encouraging him to do good;
  c) by seeing that he receives training in the arts and sciences;
  d) by finding a suitable wife for him;
  e) by giving over their wealth to him at the right time.

West. Behind, signifying wife, whom her husband should uphold in five

ways:
   a) by praising her and upholding the relationship of her truly being his wife;
   b) by not despising her or looking down on her;
   c) by not acting unfaithfully to her;
   d) by letting her be in charge (as of home and family);
   e) by giving her clothing and trinkets.

His wife having been upheld in the above ways should then help her husband in five ways:
   a) by organizing their affairs well;
   b) by helping her husband's relatives and friends;
   c) by not acting unfaithfully to her husband;
   d) by looking after the valuables and property which her husband has managed to collect;
   e) by being energetic and not lazy in all her duties.

North. The left, signifying friends, good people whom one should uphold in five ways:
   a) by sharing things with them;
   b) by talking pleasantly with them;
   c) by doing things that are useful;
   d) by being even-minded and without pride;
   e) by not speaking pretentiously and departing from what is true.

One's friends having been upheld in the above ways, should then help one in five ways:
   a) by giving protection when one has been careless;
   b) by protecting one's goods and valuables when one is careless;
   c) by giving one shelter when there is danger;
   d) by not abandoning one at a time of adversity;
   e) by upholding one including one's relatives.[13]

While the above presentation does not by any means exhaust the discussion of classical Buddhist teachings found in the curriculum, it does give an indication of their range and type. We now move to the second side of our proposition, namely, the behavior deemed ideally appropriate to the Thai society and nation.

Thai customs and culture, as previously diagrammed, are seen to be dependent on Buddhism. Such facets of the culture as a gentle and modest temperament, respectful and reverent behavior, politeness in welcoming guests, and the custom of practising merit (*puñña*) are to be preserved for the happiness of individuals and the progress of the nation.[14] The individual is taught in the ethics curriculum to be punctual in the performance of his responsibilities, to be honest, associate with good people, to be polite and modest, practice loving kindness (*metta-karuṇā*), to be generous, industrious, brave and thrifty. Good behavior in society is said to consist of following traditional Thai customs and morality, behaving respectfully, speaking politely so as not to cause dissension and unhappiness, helping the weak, behaving in a quiet and orderly manner, having the proper respect for the status of others, being pleasant and not cross or ugly, being unselfish, and not praising yourself at the expense of others.[15]

While these teachings give us a general picture of expected or normative behavior of the individual in Thai society, they do not fill in those categories depicted as particular expressions of Thai culture informed by Buddhism, namely, morality, legal rights, physical rights and social unity. Completing this enterprise will further enchance our knowledge of the way in which religio-ethical teachings support the socio-political order.

The *sīla-dhamma* text used in grades one through seven delineates morality (*khati-dhamma*) in terms of the following behavior: in whatever undertaking one engages consider the welfare of the nation; honesty, a sense of propriety, fairness, punctuality, a sense of duty; gratitude and thankfulness; being aware of the virtue of the nation and not dishonoring it; conscientious hard work, patience and frugality; acting according to one's duty; being polite, modest and with good manners; being generous and listening to the opinion of others; supportive and self-giving, loving and kind; orderly in thinking and working; a sense of unity with others in defeat and victory.[16] The other categories are presented somewhat more briefly. Legal rights (*neta-dhamma*) is the guarantee of place and position including the right of ownership and right of speech; fulfilling one's responsibility as a human being, i.e., self-preservation, propagation, obeying the law, and respecting the rights and duties of others. Physical rights (*watthu-dhamma*) include sufficient and proper food to guarantee strong bodily development and the prevention of disease; an adequate place to live; appropriate and clean clothes; sufficient health care. The last category, *saha-dhamma* or social unity is defined as knowing the right behavior and manners appropriate to Thai society. It includes such advice as how to act as a guest, how to receive a guest, manners appropriate at a party, proper behavior at a funeral, and even the admonition to walk politely on public streets.[17]

Religious and ethical instruction at the Wat Haripuñjaya boys' school and other schools throughout the country as described above attempts to provide a moral-ethical base for the socio-political order in the following ways: a structural inter-relationship between Buddhism and Thai culture; the identification of the happiness of the individual with the well-being of the nation; and the advocacy of those qualities and modes of behavior most conducive to social harmony and cohesiveness.

The Western reader may be particularly struck by the emphasis on politeness, respect, self-giving — those attitudes and actions characterized in Thai by the term *kreng chai* (i.e., politeness out of respect usually associated with an inferior-superior relationship). While many specific Buddhist ethical teachings, e.g., not taking life, are very much a part of Thai culture, qualities of *kreng chai*-ness (i.e., politeness, deference, patience, endurance) assumed to be typical of the Thai character in the *sīla-dhamma* curriculum might, indeed, be reflective of the strong Buddhist emphasis on self-lessness, non-self assertiveness, and equanimity. Such moral and behavioral qualities have abetted social cohesion both in the days of the absolute monarchy and since the 1932 coup when Thailand has been governed by aristocratic, military, and business elites. To overstate the case, it is debatable whether the kind of behavioral rationale traditionally associated with Thai Buddhist culture and identified almost completely with the Thai nation will be compatible with the political forces which have been gathering momentum in Thailand since the student uprising of October 14, 1973, which led to the ouster of the Prime Minister and two of the most powerful military figures in the country. It should also be noted that the three ousted leaders had lost their legitimacy because they had, in the students' view, acted unethically. This unethical activity justified extraordinary behavior in the students' eyes. Thus it was argued that their own behavior which was outside traditional patterns was, in fact, being loyal to the nation.

This query takes us beyond the intention of this chapter,[18] but anyone who has studied traditional Thai Buddhism and who is also aware of the most recent political events cannot help but be impressed by the contrast between the ideal citizen depicted in the religious studies literature and the activity of radical student groups, in particular. Editorials in the *Prachāthipatai* (*Democracy*), one of Thailand's most outspoken newspapers, have almost totally ruled out *kreng chai*-ness for a model of aggressive, involved activity on the part of young people directly attempting to challenge the *status quo*. Where the current political turmoil in Thailand will eventually lead is difficult to predict; at this point some kind of conflict may well emerge between the traditional support the Buddhist moral order has rendered for the socio-political order and the new style of citizen. To dramatize this conflict, we shall conclude this section with two translations, an interpretation of a *sīla-dhamma* proverb and an editorial from the *Prachāthipatai*.

One of the traditional methods of study in Thailand has been through the use of proverbs or sayings (*suphasit*). The *dhamma-su'ksā*, for example, devotes an entire volume to pithy sayings which teach not only Buddhist wisdom but the rudiments of a Pāli vocabulary as well. All of the *sīla-dhamma* books have a concluding *suphasit* section expounding various teachings such as the virtue of patience, that gratitude is a sign of a good person, that only the individual can save himself, and so on. One of the sayings particularly relevant to the issue joined in this chapter on the inter-relationship of the religious and socio-political order as seen through the medium of religious education is: *sukhā saṅgkhassa sāmaggī*. (The unity of the group is happiness). The author of this saying was a former head of the Thai Sangha, Somdet Phra Sangharāja Pussadeva, who composed it as a reminder to all Thais about the importance of social unity, of doing one's duty, and of the progress and development of the country.[19] The following is a free rendering of his commentary:

> Harmony means being united in purpose and aim (*phrọm phriang*), being together, following one's duty in the group . . .
>
> If people who live in any kind of group — family, village, town or nation — are to be satisfied and live in unity they must be united in a common aim. Social harmony depends on this kind of unity. This is not the identical kind of action you see when boy scouts or soldiers are marching and turning right, left or doing an about-face altogether. This kind of simultaneous activity is only a product of the occasion and does not evidence social harmony. Such unity depends upon everyone's working according to his individual responsibility. If the individuals in the family do not carry out their own duties, there is bound to be a problem, but if they do, happiness will prevail.
>
> In a school, if a teacher does not carry out the job of teaching, the students will be indolent and will not be encouraged in the right way. Or, if the students are not willing to work, then the school is not really a school. However, if the teacher does his duty and the students behave and really put forth an effort then the school will be what a school ought to be and everything will be satisfactory.
>
> If the people of a village, town or nation do not do their duty towards one another, if they are shirkers and procrastinators, then work will suffer. Or, if the people do not pay their taxes, the government cannot do its work and a cooperative spirit will be destroyed. But, if the people do what they are supposed to do and do their work on time, if the farmers will be farmers, artisans be artisans, businessmen be businessmen, civil servants be civil servants, policemen be policemen, then the country will be unified and there will be happiness and progress because of this harmony. Wherever there is unity, there is progress. A single thread has no power but joined together with others makes a useful rope; a small piece of wood has little value but joined with lumber makes a large house.
>
> In the time of the Buddha, King Ajāttasatrū decided to conquer the city of Vesālī in the region of the Vajjīs. He sent his army to take over the city but because the people of Vesālī were so united they were able to withstand the attack and the army of King Ajāttasatrū was repulsed. The King decided to try to defeat them by deceit. He sent a spy into the town who worked to incite the Vajjīs against each other, thereby breaking down their social cohesion and common purpose. The spy sent word to Ajāttasatrū of the disunity in the town and Ajāttassatrū sent his army again. This time they were successful because the Vajjīs were divided.
>
> A piece of machinery is made of separate parts each with its own role. If any part is broken the instrument cannot be used, but if all parts are performing their roles properly, the instrument works properly. Similarly, our bodies are made up of many different organs performing different functions. Our very lives depend upon these parts working together in harmony and unity.

The editorial pages of the *Prachāthipatai* newspaper are often filled with comments about the problems confronting Thailand and the efforts of students to correct them. At a time when public support for student involvement in the cause of the rights of laborers and farmers has declined from the halcyon days of October 14, the *Prachāthipatai* continues to espouse a student-activist point of view. The following brief excerpt is taken from the editorial of July 30, 1974:

> In the past students were taught, "The duty of students is to study. They should not criticize the government which no longer has Thanom, Praphas, and Narong [the former Prime Minister and military strong men ousted in the October 14th uprising]. Demonstrations by workers and farmers [strongly supported by activist student groups]

create disturbances in the society. While there are problems, the government is trying its best to correct them. Be understanding and join with them. Finally, the civil servants, police and military might be a bit heavy-handed, but it is necessary for the peace and order of the people. Please have more of a sense of community (*sāmaggī*)."

A feeling of "they deserve it" among the present student generation arises because they see their own disruptive activities as necessary to help the people become aware of legitimate faults in the structure of Thai society. However, after attacking (the ills of society) for a long time, they are severely criticized in the capitalist press, and among the civil service, police, and military. The students realize that this criticism aims to silence them.

After the October 14 uprising several of the activist student leaders were briefly ordained into the monkhood as a sign, one supposes, of their loyalty to Buddhism and to the country and to make merit for their deceased colleagues. One wonders, however, what changes traditional symbols of loyalty and the traditional expression of Buddhist moral support for the socio-political order will have to undergo in the face of strident calls for reformation of that order. Will the Wat Haripuñjaya boys' school and others like it around the country take seriously their potential roles in the readjustment of the various facets of the Buddhist symbol system to an all too rapidly changing socio-political order? Such tensions between the normative teachings of a religion and its institutional reality which characterize all religious traditions become more dramatic in times of profound social and cultural transition. Thai Buddhism, embroiled in the conflicts of a largely rural, traditional society moving toward modernity, finds itself having to fashion appropriate responses to new and challenging situations. We have tried to suggest only one dimension of this problem by focusing on the traditional system of religious education exemplified by Wat Haripuñjaya and juxtaposing it with some recent events which point to potential and actual areas of conflict. Before commenting on the general methodological issue relevant to the problem raised, we turn to a brief discussion of the Pāli school at the Wat.

The Pāli School

The second major educational institution at Wat Haripuñjaya is the school exclusively for Pāli and *nāga-dhamma* studies or the *rong rien pariyata-dhamma*. Monks and novices who study at this school do not engage in formal secular studies as is the case with their counterparts at the boys' school. Rather, they devote all of their formal education to religious studies and, more particularly, to the study of Pāli. Since the school was founded four years ago there has been a concerted effort at the Wat to encourage Pāli studies in Lamphun Province. The head of the school claims with some pride that in terms of numbers of monks and novices in study and examinations passed, Pāli studies in the Province surpass every other northern province including Chiang Mai. For the past three years the number of students has held fairly constant at close to one hundred, all of whom are fully supported by Wat Haripuñjaya. They come from every district in the province and also from nearby Chiang Mai, Lampang, and Mae Hong Son Provinces as well as three privinces in the northeastern part of the country.

No discussion of education at Wat Haripuñjaya can ignore the place of Pāli studies at the Wat and, indeed, throughout Thai Buddhism. Obviously, study of Pāli, the canonical language of Theravāda Buddhism, has its primary value in the enhancement of Buddhism with apparently little relevance for the socio-political realm. Yet, to the extent that Thailand and Thai Buddhism are nearly mystically identified, Pāli, the language of Buddhism, does have a peculiar significance for the thrust of the previous section. Linguistically, the corollary of the equation between being a Thai and being a Buddhist is that to understand the profundities of the Thai language one must understand Pāli. We shall return to this point after a brief examination of the nature of Pāli studies in Thailand.

The formal study of Pāli in Thailand on a national basis goes back at least three hundred years to the Ayudhayā period[20], although there is reason to assume on the basis of Pāli texts in northern *wat* libraries that particular centers of Pāli study existed in Lānnā Thai at least five hundred years ago. The Ayudhayā curriculum followed selections from the traditional divisions of Sutta, Vinaya, and Abhidhamma. During the reign of Rama II or around 1816 A.D. the Thai *sangharāja* divided Pāli studies into nine grades or levels and, while the content of each grade has changed through the years, the nine grades have been consistently maintained. In northern Thailand the standardization of Pāli studies after the central Thai model did not begin until a century later during Vajirañāṇa's tenure as head of the Sangha. The candidate stood before the examining committee holding a lighted candle. He passed if he was able to translate the passage from the Pāli text given to him before the candle burned down.[21] This was changed to standardized written examinations given at particular times throughout the country over the prescribed content for each grade.

The present curriculum is as follows:

Levels I& II
    1. The Pāli grammar of Vajirañāṇa
    2. Translating the *gathā* of the *Dhammapadaṭṭhakathā*, Books 1-4
Level III
    1. Translating the *Dhammapadaṭṭhakathā*, Books 5-8
    2. The Pāli grammar of Vajirañāṇa
Level IV
    1. Translate from Thai into Pāli the *Dhammapadaṭṭhakathā*, Book 1
    2. Translate from Pāli into Thai the *Manggalatthadīpani*, Book 1
Level V
    1. Translate from Thai into Pāli the *Dhammapadaṭṭhakathā*, Books 1-4
    2. Translate from Pāli into Thai the *Manggalatthadīpani*, Book 2
Level VI

1. Translate from Thai into Pāli the *Dhammapadaṭṭhakathā*, Books 5-8
2. Translate from Pāli into Thai the *Samantapāsādika*, Books 2, 4, 5
Level VII
1. Translate from Thai into Pāli the *Maṅggalatthadīpani*
2. Translate from Pāli into Thai the *Samantapāsādika*, Books 1 & 2
Level VIII
1. Write three kinds of poetry (out of six) in Pāli
2. Translate from Thai into Pāli the *Samantapāsādika*, Books 1 & 2
3. Translate from Pāli into Thai the *Visuddhimagga*
Level IX
1. Write in Pāli anything the committee chooses
2. Translate from Thai into Pāli the *Visuddhimagga*
3. Translate from Pāli into Thai the *Abhidhammatthavibhāvina*[22]

The Pāli curriculum, as we see above, is based almost entirely on commentarial literature, three texts by Buddhagosha or ascribed to him — the *Dhammapadaṭṭhakathā*, *Samantapāsādika* (commentary on the Vinaya), and *Visuddhimagga* — an Abhidhamma commentary, and a commentary on the *Maṅggala Sutta* written by one of the most famous northern Thai monks, Sirimangalācārya, in 1524. This text marks the high water point of Pāli works authored in Thailand. Considered by northern Thai Buddhists as one of the most perfect syntheses of Buddhist teachings every constructed, the *Maṅgaladīpanī* comments on the thirty-eight auspicious acts advocated in the *Maṅgala Sutta* ranging from not associating with the unwise to the attainment of Nibbāna.[23] It intertwines popular moral fables with abstract doctrinal teachings after the manner of the finest Theravāda commentarial literature and is justly admired throughout the Theravāda world. Indeed, the work is of such a high quality that Sinhalese Buddhists are wont to claim that Sirimangalācārya was not a northern Thai but a Sinhalese!

The study of Pāli represents the very essence or heart of Theravāda Buddhism, throughout Thailand. Historically, Pāli study in northern Thailand attained to a high level as evidenced by the fact that the majority of original Pāli works by Thai monks were written there. Since it is widely assumed that Pāli was Magadhi, the language of the Buddha, to know Pāli not only denotes the ability to better understand Buddhist teachings but is charged with the sacredness of the Buddha himself. As Tambiah so well points out, the sacrality of Pāli is especially apparent in the meritorious and protective effect attending chanting services is believed to have.[24] Thus, knowledge of Pāli is charged with the sacred chrisma of the Buddha himself, is necessary for an adequate understanding of the teachings of the Buddha (*Buddha-vācana*), and is an essential part of most Buddhist ceremonies where words function as the primary medium of sacred power.

Informants offer additional reasons for the study of Pāli such as: the health and well-being of Buddhism are tied to the study of Pāli since knowing the language of the *Buddha-vācana* increases understanding and eliminates doubt; it has the moral value of encouraging qualities of patience, endurance and a care for detail; it abets pride in the region since many of the most important Pāli works of Thailand were written there; and, a profound understanding of Thai demands the study of Pāli. As mentioned above, the connection between Pāli and Thai reinforces the sense of identity between Buddhism and Thai-ness. Perhaps on the verbal level it is no exaggeration to claim that Pāli symbolizes that which is most sacred in the religion and the nation, and that knowledge of Pāli penetrates more deeply the depth of Thai-Buddhist self-identity. The high regard for attainment in Pāli proficiency evidences itself both in terms of the general respect informed laymen have for those monks who have passed the highest levels of Pāli examination and the honor paid to them in the Sangha itself. Thus, every monk who passes the third level of Pāli studies is entitled to be called *Phra-mahā* rather than merely *Phra*, and upon the occasion of passing grades six and nine is presented with a special fan donated by the king himself. Consequently, Wat Haripuñjaya is justly proud of the fact that Pāli studies are on the upswing at the Wat, that in the current year (1974 A.D.) there are six students studying at the fourth level, and that several have passed the exams for grades six and seven.

In this chapter we have described but two facets of Wat Haripuñjaya as an educational center — the boys' school and the school exclusively for religious and Pāli studies. Other aspects of Wat education such as the evening adult school under the aegis of the boys' school or the instruction which takes place at the various meetings throughout the year have not been discussed. Our purpose in focusing exclusively on the two major educational institutions at the Wat has been to explicate the particular ways in which education helps establish both the moral basis of the socio-political order (*ānācakra*) and the sacrality of the religious realm (*sāsanacakra*). The boys' school, in particular, symbolizes the inter-connection between the two, while the school for Pāli studies serves — in much the same way as the sacred pre-history of the Wat and the cycle of major Buddhist ceremonies — to establish the religious realm firmly in relationship to the founder of the tradition.

As an addendum to our discussion of the *pāli-dhamma* curriculum we noted the possibility of conflict between the traditional moral justification of the socio-political realm and demands for reform on the part of student activists. While the perspective throughout this study has been on order rather than disorder this addendum affords the opportunity of making an observation about the binary categories of order/disorder, cosmos/chaos, structure/anti-structure.[25] A binary dynamic tension is not absent from the various facets of Wat Haripuñjaya we have examined. There is the opposition of hilltribe-barbarian/city-cultured in the founding of Haripuñjaya, the carnival/rite polarity in the Wat's annual festival, and in this chapter the tension between conventional social roles and moral behavior and the implicit critique of those roles and behavior by student activists. In the first, the mythic-legend appears to resolve the polarity by designating specific locations within the borders of the town for both indigenous and cultured constituents; in the second, carnival acts as prelude to rite; and the third is still in process leaving the shape of its future resolution unclear. Whether or not the Sangha will be able to enter creatively into the resolution of this opposition will depend to a large degree on its ability to rise above the particularized and parochialized situation from the perspective of the universal dimension of its ideological structure.[26] In terms of Clifford Geertz's analysis of religion as a cultural system,[27] the more particularized ("model for") dimensions of the symbol system of Thai Buddhism will have to take on re-specification both in terms of teaching and practice if the Thai Sangha is to retain a dynamic viability for the future. Such redefinition, I am convinced, cannot be left merely to the whim of history but calls for wise and insightful leadership. The ideological structure of Thai Buddhism has the potential for helping to lift both the Sangha and the nation beyond the limits of Thailand's current tensions precisely because that dimension of Thai Buddhism (the universal or "model-of" dimension) has never been simply identified with the ideological structures of the country; or, metaphorically, we might say that the two wheels of Dhamma have never been totally identified one with the other. Paradoxically, to the degree Thai Buddhism has existed in tension with its cultural society, to that degree it may now have the potential to participate in the process of its own reformation and even the reformation of the nation.

---

[1]See Frank Reynolds, "The Two Wheels of Dhamma: A Study of Early Buddhism," *The Two Wheels of Dhamma: Essays on the Theravada Tradition in India and Ceylon*, ed. Bardwell L. Smith, AAR Studies in Religion, no. 3 (Chambersburg: American Academy of Religion, 1972) for an analysis of the interaction of these two orders in the Indian Buddhist tradition.

[2]Koson Srisang discusses the interrelationship between Thai Buddhism and the Thai nation-state since 1932 in his University of Chicago PhD dissertation *Dhammacracy in Thailand: A Study in Social Ethics as a Hermeneutic of Dhamma* (1973).

[3]1973 statistics provided by the Office of Education, Lamphun Province.

[4]1974 statistics provided by the head-teacher (*kru yai*) of the Wat Haripuñjaya boys' school *(Rong Rien Mettī).*

[5]The Buddhist studies curriculum is divided into three grades. It is coordinated with Pāli studies only to the extent that the monk or novice who has passed Pāli degrees II and III must have passed *nāga dhamma* I; Pāli degree IV must have passed *nāga dhamma* II; and Pāli degree VII must have passed *nāga dhamma* III.

[6]It seems generally to be the case throughout the country that study of *sīla-dhamma* is taken less seriously than other academic subjects.

[7]Based on the text from primary grades: *Baep Rian Sangkhom Su'ksā Wichā Sīla-dhamma Prayok Prathom Su'ksā Ton Plāi* (Social Studies Curriculum. Ethics for Primary Grades), (Bangkok: Ministry of Education, 1973).

[8]*Ibid.*, pp. 34-35.

[9]*Ibid.*, p. 26. Also Vajirañāṇa, *Navakovāda* (Bangkok: Mahā Makuta Buddhist University, 1971), p. 84.

[10]*Ethics for Primary Grades*, pp. 26-27.

[11]*Baep Rian . . . Chan Mathayom Suk'ksā Pī Tī 1* (Ethics for the First Secondary Grade), (Bangkok: Ministry of Education, 1973), p. 53.

[12]*Navakovāda*, pp. 77-91.

[13]*Ibid.*, pp. 86-88.

[14]*Ethics for Primary Grades*, pp. 91-93.

[15]*Ibid.*, pp. 89-90.

[16]*Ibid.*, pp. 94-95.

[17]*Ibid.*, pp. 94-99.

[18]The Sangha is making various kinds of adjustments to social and political changes in Thailand. Two of the most striking developments are in the areas of Buddhist higher education, especially Mahāchulālongkorn Buddhist University in Bangkok, and the establishment of community development training programs for monks. (See my "Community Development and Thai Buddhism," *Visakha Puja 2516*, Bangkok: Buddhist Assoc., 1973, pp. 59-67.) In a forthcoming article Frank Reynolds discusses the relationship between the religious and socio-political orders specifically in relationship to the October 14, 1973, uprising. Our use of this contemporary example is partially intended to suggest the interpretative perspective of binary oppositions mentioned briefly at the end of this chapter which our interpretative model is not intended to encompass.

[19]*Baep Rian . . . Chan Mathayom Su'ksa Pī Tī 2* (Ethics for the Second Secondary Grade), (Bangkok: Ministry of Education, 1973), pp. 180-86.

[20]Phramahā Sarachet, "Kan su'ksā Chan Udom Su'ksā Khong Khana Sangkha Thai Yuk Paccupan" (Higher Education in the Thai Sangha in the Modern Period). Xerox copy. Source unknown, p. 85.

[21]*Ibid.*, p. 87.

[22]*Ibid.*, pp. 91-92.

[23]S. J. Tambiah, *Buddhism and the Spirit Cults . . .* , p. 214.

[24]*Ibid.*, pp. 195ff.

[25]For example, the liminality/communities typology Victor W. Turner sets up (*The Ritual Process, Structure and Anti-Structure*, Chicago: Aldine Publishing Co., 1969) would be a very provocative perspective from which to analyze the behavior of those student leaders who entered the Sangha after the radically disruptive episode of October 14, 1973, even though it would be stretching these categories far beyond Van Gennep's and Victor Turner's contexts.

[26]Robert Bellah's analysis of the relationship between religion and society ("Epilogue: Religion and Progress in Modern Asia," *Religion and Progress in Modern Asia*, ed. Robert N. Bellah, Glencoe: The Free Press, 1965) has been particularly useful to my own thinking on this subject. See my *Buddhism in Transition* (Philadelphia: Westminster Press, 1969).

[27]Clifford Geertz, "Religion As A Cultural System," *Reader in Comparative Religion: An Anthropological Approach*, 2nd ed., eds. William A. Lessa and Evon Z. Vogt (New York: Harper & Row), pp. 204-15.

Chapter V

The Wat as Administrative Center

Throughout this study we have taken the position that Wat Haripuñjaya is the symbolic center of a sacred religious realm into which the socio-political realm is assimilated on a variety of levels. The centrality of the Wat from a functional point of view becomes quite clear when we see it administratively in relationship to the highly structured organization of the Thai Sangha. Rather than beginning with the organization of the Thai national Sangha, however, recently discussed by Jane Bunnag and earlier by Kenneth Wells,[1] we propose first to examine the internal organization of Wat Haripuñjaya and then through its central administrators illustrate the ways it is linked with the national, regional, provincial, and district organization of the monastic order. Finally, we shall turn to a comparison between ecclesiastical and governmental structures and one mode of inter-relationship, the national *Dhammadhuta* program in which Wat Haripuñjaya, through its abbot, has played a major role.

Organization and Leadership

The final power and authority of Wat Haripuñjaya, as is true for every other Thai *wat* is the abbot (*chao avāsa*). In the case of larger *wats* the abbot will have a formally designated assistant (*rǫng chao avāsa*). Wat Haripuñjaya's size and four-fold *sanghavāsa* makes for a slightly more elaborate internal administrative structure which can be diagrammed as follows:

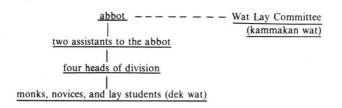

81

Theoretically the chief administrative structure of the Wat could consist of six monks. In fact, as is presently the case, with overlapping responsibilities the total number is smaller. Currently the abbot and his two assistants are also heads of *sanghavāsa* divisions and, in fact, these three monks wield the principal authority in the Wat. They are also three of the most important administrators in the province. We shall now look briefly at their histories and their roles.[3]

The abbot of Wat Haripuñjaya, Phra Dhammamōlī through position and seniority is currently the most prestigious ecclesiastical official in northern Thailand. Born in 1910 (B.E. 2453) in Ayudhyā Province, central Thailand, he has spent nearly his entire life since the age of nine in the Sangha. Having completed his primary education at Wat Pai Bua he went to Bangkok to live with relatives when he was thirteen and studied Pāli grammar for a year at the age of fifteen (1925). Continuing his study of Pāli and *Buddha-dhamma* he passed the third Pāli grade and first level of *nāga dhamma* studies (Buddhist history and doctrine) in 1927; two years later he successfully completed the fourth Pāli grade and second *nāga dhamma* level; and in 1930 at the age of 20 he passed the fifth Pāli grade.

Phra Dhammamōlī's monastic home during his fifteen years in Bangkok was Wat Benjamabopitr, the beautiful Marble Temple, built by King Chulalongkorn (Rama V). He was ordained a monk there in 1931 (B.E. 2474) at the age of twenty-one. His diligence for study continued unabated leading to the sixth Pāli grade in 1932, and the seventh Pāli grade and final *nāga dhamma* level in 1935. Even while a novice his scholastic ability was recognized and in 1930 he began teaching Pāli at the Wat. Three years later he was appointed as a member of the national examination committee for *nāga dhamma* and Pāli studies further enhancing his prestige in the circles of ecclesiastical studies.

Wat Benjamabopitr has had a long-standing connection with northern Thailand which may account for the fact that in 1938 Phra Dhammamōlī moved to Wat Haripuñjaya where he continued his role as teacher of Pāli. His advancement through various offices in Lamphun Province and the northern region was rapid and deserves specific enumeration: appointed as the assistant to the ecclesiastical head of Lamphun District in 1940, a position he held for eight years; head of ecclesiastical education in the Province (1944); *upajjāya*[4] for Lamphun Province, 1944; elevated to be the Abbot of Wat Haripuñjaya, 1946; assistant to the ecclesiastical head of Regions Four and Five, 1948; interim ecclesiastical head of Lamphun Province, 1963; assistant ecclesiastical head of Region Seven (Lamphun, Chiangmai, and Mae Hong Son Provinces), 1964; ecclesiastical head of Region Seven, 1965; director of the *Dhammadhuta* (see following section) Program for Division Four (Lamphun, Chiangmai, Mae Hong Son, Lampang, Prae, Nan, Chiangrai Provinces), 1973.

These wide-spread responsibilities have been duly recognized by the national ecclesiastical authorities and since the age of 36 when he was made abbot of Wat Haripuñjaya he has held various titles within the highest range of ecclesiastical rank known as *phra racha chana* but more commonly referred to as *chao khun* ("my lord"). There are over forty different ranks in the Thai Buddhist Sangha ranging from the common denominator *phra*, the title for all who have received ordination into the monkhood, to *sangha-rāja* or head of the Thai Sangha who bears the title *Phra Somdet Sangharāja*. The forty odd ranks are divided into four major divisions: *phra*, *phra mahā*, *phra khru*, and *phra racha khana*.[5] Ranks are conferred for a variety of reasons including seniority, function, ability, and favoritism. We have already indicated that every monk who passes the third Pāli level automatically becomes a *phra mahā*. Beyond that level, however, educational qualifications are much less important than ecclesiastical function or role, and whether or not one is liked and admired by his superiors and peers. Recommendations for change in rank are made through the ecclesiastical hierarchy. Suffice it to say here that ranks of *phra khru* grade and above are approved through a sequence moving from the Wat to the district, province, region, and finally to the Supreme Sangha Council and the King. The close relationship between ecclesiastical ranking and the state or the socio-political order is symbolized by the honorific fans presented by the King for grades of *phra khru* and above.

Having examined the development of the career of the abbot of Wat Haripuñjaya, we move now to a consideration of his role as abbot, head of Region Seven, and director of the *Dhammadhuta* for Division Four.

Phra Dhammamōlī's functions as abbot may be divided into four major areas: supervisions of the monks and novices, education, propagation, and general oversight of the Wat. Each of these areas entails some of the following responsibilities: 1) supervision of the monks and novices — to establish the rules for monks, novices, and students living at the Wat; to look after the general welfare of the monks, novices, and students; to see that they receive the proper medical care when ill; to ensure that everyone at the Wat is being properly nourished; and, to provide for the convenience of the lay people who attend the Wat; 2) education — support the school for Pāli and Buddhist studies and the Haripuñjaya boys' school; arrange for instructing the laity in Buddhist thought and practice including instruction in meditation; and, encouragement of the adult education program under the aegis of the boys' school; 3) propagation (*phoei phrae*) — meetings for monks, novices, and students living at the Wat; preaching sermons at sabbath services and other meetings for the laity; arranging for celebrations on special Buddhist holy days; encouraging the activities of the Buddhist adult fellowship and youth organization; 4) general oversight — repair and renovation of the *ceitya*-reliquary, the various *vihāra* and Buddha images; building new buildings for the schools, monks' quarters, and meeting pavilions.

Phra Dhammamōlī's role as ecclesiastical head of Region (*phāk*) Seven may be delineated in terms of the same four categories: 1) supervision of monks and novices — general oversight of all the monks and novices in the Region; calming any altercations that might arise; encouraging members of the Sangha in positions of authority; joining laity in looking after the monks and novices in the region; encouraging order in the Sangha through obedience to the national Sangha law and legal statutes; 2) education — to preserve and encourage the study of Pāli and Buddhist subjects; to visit the examination centers for Pāli and *nāga dhamma*; to send teachers to meet the needs of the Pāli/*nāga dhamma* schools; 3) propagation — to meet with monks, novices and laity in rural villages in order to preach, instruct in right behavior, and teach meditation; 4) general oversight — to give advice on the building and care of *wat* buildings and compounds.

The national *Dhammadhuta* program integrating instruction in Buddhist doctrine and ethics with government programs for health, public welfare, and community development was begun nearly 20 years ago. While we shall examine in some detail the nature of this program and its implications for the inter-relationship between the religious (*sāsanacakra*) and socio-political (*ānācakra*) realms, a brief description of Phra Dhammamōlī's role as head of the *Dhammadhuta* for Division (*sai*) Four will complete this presentation of the duties and responsibilities of the abbot of Wat Haripuñjaya. In this capacity Phra Dhammamōlī approves the appointment of monks in all seven of the northern provinces to be designated as Dhammadhuta representatives to go out into every district, sub-district, and village to meet with the people. In 1973, the first year he was given this responsibility, he personally chaired a ten-day meeting of monks, novices, government officials, teachers, soldiers, students, and farmers in Nan province, one of the less developed of the northern provinces with a considerable insurgency problem.

Since the responsibilities of the abbot of Wat Haripuñjaya inevitably involve administrative relationships with the national Sangha and the government our analysis will be delayed until we have presented the careers and roles of the two assistants to the abbot, Phra Khru Sōphon and Phra Khru Prasāt, two important leaders within the Wat, district, and province.

Unlike the abbot, both of his assistants are northerners. Phra Khru Sōphon was born in 1924 (B.E. 2467) in Lamphun Province. His ordination as a novice at the age of fourteen and as a monk at the age of twenty-one both took place at Wat Haripuñjaya. At the time of this writing (1974) he has completed a total of thirty-five years as a member of the Sangha. Within the Wat he has four major areas of responsibility: 1) assistant to the abbot — special responsibilities are in the areas of education and propagation (*phoei phrae*) entailing in particular the conduct of ceremonies (*sāsanā phithī*) and preaching (*sadaeng phra-dhamma-desanā*); 2) head of one of the four Sangha divisions (i.e., *Attharasa*) — has the responsibility for seeing that the monks, novices and *dek wat* (young boys who perform services for the *wat* in exchange for room and board) obey the Vinaya and the rules of the Wat, and for instructing them in taking responsibility for making adjustments within the patterns of the division; 3) the head teacher (*khru yai*) in charge of religious instruction — acts as a consultant for instructors teaching Buddhist subjects at the Wat, arranges for teachers offering religious instruction in the Wat's schools, instructs monks and novices in their responsibilities toward the Sangha and society, and teaches classes for which teachers cannot be found; 4) head of the Pāli/*nāga dhamma* school — arranges for students to teach Buddhist morals and ethics at various *wats* as requested by the Sangha or the government; instruction in ethics and doctrine at various schools, T.V. and radio lectures on Buddhism, editor of *Santisukha* magazine published four times per year by Wat Haripuñjaya. In relationship to the national Sangha organization Phra Khru Sōphon plays two major roles: as ecclesiastical secretary of Lamphun Province he handles the correspondence of the head of the Province (*chao khana chang wat*); records any minutes dealing with discipline, education, propagation, or the lay public; and functions as a consultant for the ecclesiastical head of the Province; furthermore, as assistant to the ecclesiastical head of the District (*chao khana amphur*) he fulfills whatever jobs are assigned to him regarding education and propagation in particular.

Phra Khru Sōphon's close friend, Phra Khru Prasāt, has shared a similar career of long tenure in the Sangha and now occupies a position of singular import within the internal administration of Wat Haripuñjaya and the work of the Sangha on the district and provincial levels. Born in the town of Lamphun in 1926 (B.E. 2469), Phra Khru Prasāt was ordained a novice at the age of twelve and a monk at the age of twenty-one at Wat Haripuñjaya. He received his primary education in Lamphun before his novitiate ordination after which time he completed his *nāga dhamma* studies between 1937 and 1945. His responsibilities include being the head of one of the four *Sanghavāsa* divisions of Wat Haripuñjaya, one of the two assistants to the abbot, one of the *upajjhāya* (i.e., one authorized to ordain) for the district of Lamphun, and the ecclesiastical head of Lamphun district (*chao khana amphur*). As assistant to the abbot his primary responsibility lies in the area of helping to arrange for the rituals and festivals which take place at the Wat, e.g., the annual Wat festival, the *Thet Mahā-chat*. As the head of Lamphun District he has general supervision over the 367 monks and 1577 novices resident in the 145 *wats* located within Lamphun's eighteen sub-districts. He carries out this role with the help of the ecclesiastical heads of the sub-districts and the *wat* abbots, assuming responsibility for problems of discipline and education which are within the purview of the *chao khana amphur*. Other aspects of his role as ecclesiastical district head include: propagation — arranging for lectures and discussions at various *wats* with the help of students and teachers at *wat* schools; education — securing funds to support Pāli and *nāga dhamma* studies; construction — approves plans for all *wat* buildings within the district. The most difficult problem Phra Khru Prasāt believes he faces at this time is raising funds to cover the costs of maintenance, equipment, and salaries for Pāli and *nāga dhamma* studies. In 1973 the District had a total of 176 Pāli students, 1446 monks and novices in *nāga dhamma* studies, 708 in *dhamma-su 'ksā* studies, and 89 teachers. For this considerable undertaking he has no real budget other than the interest from a small endowment. Thus, like the budget of most *wats* in the province, financial support for Buddhist studies is largely dependent upon the generosity of free-will offerings by the laity.

The three monks whose *vitae* we have briefly presented are, to be sure, among the busiest in the entire province. In addition to their formal responsibilities within Wat Haripuñjaya and the Sangha, they are literally deluged with invitations from monks and laymen to participate in special Sangha ceremonies, weddings, funerals, house dedications, and so on.[6] Unlike monks in less critical positions at rural *wats*, the abbot of Wat Haripuñjaya and his two assistants have very little free time from early morning to night. Indeed, when they are free from performing a specific task they are often in their rooms being consulted by novices residing in their division or laymen coming to seek their advice.

Within the Province of Lamphun no *wat* rivals Wat Haripuñjaya in size and complexity. Its twenty-six monks, seventy-eight novices, and forty *dek wat* are subject to the authority of the abbot and division heads. While final responsibility rests with the abbot many of the Wat's activities are delegated to the two assistants he has selected who have been duly appointed by the ecclesiastical head of the district. Within each of the four divisions of the Sanghavāsa, each division head (*chao khana*) oversees the discipline and conduct of all residents. Responsibility for correcting infractions of the rules lies initially with him, and will be carried out informally through consultation with the individual involved even to the point of calling in the boy's parents in the case of a novice. Should these informal means of correcting a discipline problem prove ineffectual then the division head has the authority to recommend dismissal from the Wat or, in the event of an infraction of one of the *pārājika* rules of the Vinaya, then expulsion from the Order.

Despite the relatively complex structure of ranks within the Sangha and an apparent concern for status, relationships within the *wat* tend to be fairly informal. Indeed, my observations at ceremonies on the district and provincial level confirm that *bhikkhu* relationships in those contexts follow a similar pattern even though deference to rank appears in such obvious situations as the order of seating when chanting. Since our principal interest is in establishing the administrative centrality of the Wat as a functional expression of its historical and symbolic importance we shall now turn to the relationship between the Wat and the national Sangha structure.

Wat Haripuñjaya and the National Sangha

We have already established Wat Haripuñjaya's crucial role in the province particularly in the field of education (see Chapter IV). From that perspective its primary administrative significance stems from the fact that through its schools the Wat has trained many of the abbots and sub-district leaders in the province. To get some idea of the actual size of the contribution Wat Haripuñjaya has made to the training of leadership within Lamphun Province we provide the following breakdown:[7]

DISTRICTS (*amphur*)	NUMBER OF WATS	NUMBER OF MONKS	NUMBER OF NOVICES	*DEK WAT*
Lamphun	145	367	1577	878
Pāsāng	67	179	761	340
Ban Hong	26	67	294	161
Lī	38	71	334	205
Mae Thā	27	49	271	120
Total	303	733	3237	1704

Out of a total of 303 *wats* Wat Haripuñjaya now has proportionately more administrative leaders than any other *wat*, has educated more monks and novices, and has contributed more to the training of ecclesiastical leaders than any other single *wat*. The above chart also points out two interesting features of northern Thai Buddhism unrelated to the thrust of this chapter; namely, that novices outnumber monks nearly five to one unlike central Thailand where monks generally outnumber novices; and, that out of a male population of 162,377 less than 2.5% are ordained. I cite this last statistic to counter critics of Buddhism who charge that the Sangha drains off a significant labor force into an unproductive vocation.

The administrative influence of Wat Haripuñjaya reaches in several directions at the same time as the presentation of the careers and roles of the three key leaders at the Wat has shown. Justified partially by history in its focal administrative role, its current functional importance rests largely with its personnel. The following diagram sets forth the contribution Wat Haripuñjaya is making to various levels of the national Sangha organization:

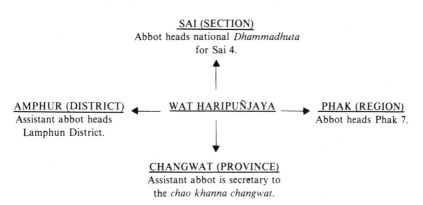

SAI (SECTION)
Abbot heads national *Dhammadhuta*
for Sai 4.

AMPHUR (DISTRICT) ◄——— WAT HARIPUÑJAYA ———► PHAK (REGION)
Assistant abbot heads   Abbot heads Phak 7.
Lamphun District.

CHANGWAT (PROVINCE)
Assistant abbot is secretary to
the *chao khanna changwat.*

Should the abbot and his assistants be of lesser ecclesiastical stature than is presently the case, claims for Wat Haripuñjaya's key administrative role might not be made so decisively. Thus, despite the role history may have intended for the Wat as a religious center, its continued value in terms of the Sangha as an institution in Thai society depends upon the ability of its leaders. They need not be famed for their spiritual accomplishments although such a reputation contributes to their personal charisma. The three leading monks at Wat Haripuñjaya are noted primarily as capable administrative leaders of the Sangha on district and provincial levels. Within the province special respect is accorded the head of the province (*chao khana cangwat*) who has attained a very venerable age, and the abbot of a *wat* in Pāsāng district noted for his spiritual qualities, strict observance of the Vinaya, and continual meditation practice. I cite these two monks to register my agreement with Jane Bunnag's rough distinction between "active" and "passive" types of Sangha leaders even though the point is only tangentially related to the argument of the chapter.[8]

The above diagram represents Wat Haripuñjaya's actual contribution to the national Sangha, or we might say that it illustrates the structure of the Sangha from the perspective of the Wat. In order, however, to get a better idea of the way in which the national Sangha relates to the state or socio-political order we must see the Sangha from the top down, as it were, rather than from the bottom up. The following diagram is based on the *Act on the Administration of the Buddhist Order of the Sangha of* B.E. *2505 (1962)*:[9]

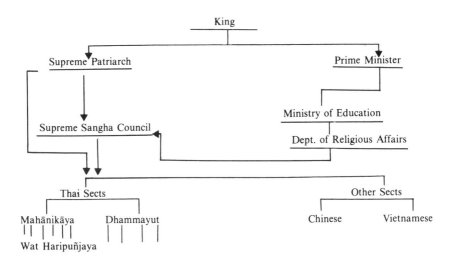

As the diagram illustrates, the king has formal authority over both the Sangha or religious order (*sāsanācakra*) and the state or socio-political order (*ānācakra*). In regard to the Sangha the king's authority is acknowledged by the fact that he gives formal approval to the selection of the head of the

Sangha (*sangharāja*) by the Supreme Sangha Council (*mahāthera samakhom*). His support of the Sangha is symbolically registered by the presentation of ceremonial fans to monks involved in various levels of the leadership of the Sangha. In effect, this means that *bhikkhu*s from the ecclesiastical status of *phra khru* on up have fans granted to them by the King. In contrast to the more flexible Sangha organization from the period of 1942 to 1962, the current Sangha structure is much more centralized[10] with final executive, legislative and judicial authority in one Supreme Sangha Council. This Council consists of the Supreme Patriarch, the Director-General of the Department of Relgious Affairs, monks of *somdet* rank (four in 1965), and four to eight monks of the *rājakhana* appointed for two-year terms. Beneath it are ranged the ecclesiastical heads responsible for the conduct of the Sangha from the largest units (i.e., sectional heads) to the smallest (i.e., *wat* abbots), each regional, provincial, district and sub-district ecclesiastical governor being under the authority of the ecclesiastical head immediately over him.

Of even more interest for our purposes than the organization of the Sangha as such is the relationship between the religious and the political orders. Formally, the two are in tandem with ecclesiastical governors on the provincial level paralleling secular governors and so on through the district and sub-district levels. Such a dual organizational scheme is not unique to Thailand. Hans-Dieter Evers has pointed out a similar type of parallel organization between the religious and political systems in Ceylon as embodied in one of the major Sinhalese temples of the Kandian period.[11] This organizational duality adds a new dimension to other binary or trinary forms that have been examined by anthropologists of Theravāda Buddhist cultures. For the most part they have been interested primarily in the structural and/or functional interrelationships between Theravāda Buddhism and Brahmanism/magical animism.[12] Our typology, like that of Evers, includes political as well as religious systems. We now turn to some of the specific ways the religious and political orders relate on the administrative level.

We have already pointed out some of the forms of interrelationship between the religious and political orders at Wat Haripuñjaya, e.g., participation by the King and government officials in critical Wat festivals, and the seeming coincidence between Buddhist moral and ethical values as taught in the school and good citizenship; however, we have yet to examine the ways in which the administrative structures interrelate. On a functional level, as the diagram illustrates, the government and the Sangha interrelate through the Department of Religious Affairs which is one of the divisions of the Ministry of Education. On the highest level we see that the Director-General of the Department of Religious Affairs sits as an advisor on the Supreme Sangha Council. Throughout the other administrative divisions of Sangha and State, the office of education at that particular level has special responsibility for the Sangha at the corresponding level. For example, most of my statistics on the number of *wat*s, monks, and novices in Lamphun

Province came from the provincial Office of Education, and even my research on Buddhism in Lamphun had to be approved by the Office of Education of the Province as well as the ecclesiastical governor.

In recent years the Ministry of Interior and the Department of Public Welfare have become directly involved in two Sangha programs. One of these programs, the *Dhammacarika*, aimed specifically at the propagation of Buddhism among tribal peoples in the northern mountainous regions, is part of the Development Program (*Dhammaphattana*) of the Ministry of Education and related to the Department of Justice of the Ministry of Interior. Both of these programs provide excellent contemporary examples of the inter-relationship between the religious and socio-political orders in Thailand and ways in which both the Sangha and the government are responding to social, economic, and political change in the country. Wat Haripuñjaya is directly involved in the *Dhammadhuta* program through its abbot who heads the program in the seven northern provinces. We propose to conclude this chapter with a brief description of a *Dhammadhuta* training session sponsored by Wat Haripuñjaya in April 1974 to provide a specific example of Sangha-government cooperation.

Referred to as Dhamma Development (*Dhammaphattana*), the project was held from April 5 to May 1 at the village of Ban Pa Phlu, Ban Hong District, Lamphun Province. The core members of the project included fifteen people, six monks, teachers and sub-district heads, in a daily regime including both instruction and practical labor. The days were spent working and the evenings listening to sermons, lectures, and discussions. During the entire month and as an expressed part of the program for the purpose of "strengthening the resolve and bringing blessings on those involved in the project" forty-nine monks dedicated themselves to follow the *dhuthanga* way (i.e., a more ascetic pattern of mendicancy than the normal monastic residency). Cooperation was received from the government and ecclesiastical heads of the district, sub-district, village headmen, abbots, businessmen and civil servants as well as the local populace who volunteered their labor.

The purpose of the work project was to repair a footbridge over the Li River approximately 40 meters by 3 1/2 meters, and repair approximately four kilometers of road. An estimated 40,000 baht or $2000 was donated for the project including food and labor estimates as well as cash. Funds remaining in the amount of over $300 were divided among the Development Committees of three local villages. The evening meetings regularly attended by around 150 people focused on some of the following topics: the purpose and aim of development; development as it applies to both material and spiritual sides of life; agricultural diversification (included distributing seeds for experimentation); instruction in public health by public health officials; and instruction in the law conducted by police officials.[14]

Dhamma Development in Thailand has several facets and is being conducted through both national and local programs.[15] While these programs vary both in quality and rationale they share the common characteristic of placing Sangha and government officials together working for a common end. Informants point out that this association helps to instill trust in the government. In effect, the Sangha mediates the role of government official and the police in Dhamma Development projects. Defenders of the *Dhammadhuta* Program are inclined to argue that Sangha involvement in development is but another and more contemporary form of the monks' traditional role in society. Its critics see the Program as a subversion of the Sangha to the purposes of the state. This latter judgment is, I believe, too harsh in the light of the parallelism between the religious and socio-political orders as presented in this chapter. However, there is a danger that as Thai society moves from traditional to more modern forms the symbolic status of the monk will be adversely affected by the ready identification made between Sangha and government officials in Dhamma Development projects. In short, in a traditional society where the perceived split between sacred and profane realms is negligible, the *bhikkhu* as a religious actor has a greater latitude of role than in an early modern or modern society where secular or profane designations are more readily made.

Administratively, Wat Haripuñjaya is currently one of the major *wat*s of northern Thailand. This position, stemming from historical precedent, also depends on the status and ability of its senior monks — the abbot and the two monastic division heads whose responsibilities we have already delineated. Through status, ecclesiastical rank, and administrative responsibility the leadership of Wat Haripuñjaya exemplifies not only the hierarchical nexus of relationships which characterize the organization of the Thai Sangha but also the parallel structure which has existed between the Sangha and the Thai nation-state in the modern period. This parallelism has served to enhance the power and prestige of the Order throughout the country, and has also helped to make Thai Buddhism one of the most pervasive social integrators within Thailand. Recognizing the value of Buddhism as a force for national integration the government has encouraged a higher degree of centralization within the Sangha through the National Sangha Law of 1968; and, furthermore, has supported programs for the upgrading of Buddhism throughout the country, has supported the association of Buddhism with programs of community development in rural areas, and the propagation of Buddhism among non-Buddhist, tribal minorities.[16] These programs are affiliated with government departments.

In the light of our analysis we see several points of administrative interaction between the religious and political realms and not always on equal terms. Symbolically the King's approval of the *sangharāja* expresses the traditional posture of the King as the defender of the Faith and also as one with a higher authority. Functionally, the presence of the Director-General of the Department of Religious Affairs on the Supreme Sangha Council and the affiliation of two nation-wide Sangha programs with government departments illustrate particular ways in which the government is involved in the support of Buddhism. While our analysis has emphasized the mutuality of this relationship both historically and contemporaneously, in Chapters I and III particular tensions in this symbiosis are mentioned.

*   *   *

The study of Wat Phra Dhātu Luang Haripuñjaya, the Royal Temple-Monastery of Haripuñjaya in Lamphun, has been a case study of institutional Buddhism in northern Thailand. We have adopted a holistic approach ranging over the Wat's history, its physical structure, ritual/festival cycle, its religious education, and, finally, its administrative nature and relationship with the Sangha and the state. Methodologically the study is eclectic; however, it is particularly indebted to the work of Frank E. Reynolds on the juxtaposition of religious (*sasanācakra*) and socio-political (*ānācakra*) orders, and to S. J. Tambiah's notion of the study of religion as a total field in its synchronic and diachronic dimensions capable of synthesis into a "kaleidoscopic view."[17] Tambiah offers a diagram of this synthesis illustrating primarily the ways in which the various levels of religious expression are integrated into a single unity. By way of conclusion I would like to set forth my own diagram consistent with the main thrust of this monograph, namely, the integration of moral-ontological, cosmic-natural, and socio-political levels of order reflected in the various symbol systems of a major Buddhist institution:

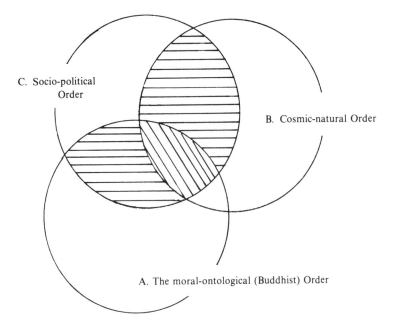

The diagram attempts to point out: 1) that the three levels of order are integrated and yet distinct; and 2) that at some points (illustrated by the vertical lines) all three orders overlap but that at other points (illustrated by the horizontal lines) the overlap is between only two of the orders. To apply this diagram to the development of the monograph itself we see that, in effect, Chapters I and II emphasize various facets of the relationship between the Buddhist and Cosmic Orders, Chapters IV and V delineate in particular the relationship between the Buddhist and Political Orders, and Chapter III presents more of an equal integration among the three Orders. Furthermore, within this development we have pointed out that symbolic and structural perspectives dominate the first three chapters and functional aspects of the study are more characteristic of the last two chapters.

This organic model has attempted to establish the nature of northern Thai Buddhism around the structural relationship among three major components. It has provided a perspective on the way in which myth and legend are related to history, how artistic and architectural form reflect a particular pattern of sacred space and the content of a religious tradition, the ways in which ritual celebration contemporize myth and legend as well as integrate socio-political realities, and the functional dimensions of the relationship between religious and secular institutions. To the extent that this study has successfully articulated these points it serves as a particular kind of exemplification of a Geertzian concept of religion as a cultural institution; to the extent the monograph presupposes that religion stands outside as well as within a culture it reflects Robert Bellah's analysis of religion in modern Asia. While at particular points this study of northern Thai Buddhism mentions a binary structural perspective of a Lévi-Straussian mode the model is not intended to cope adequately with specific sets of structural relationships in terms of the dynamic of opposition and resolution. Consequently, a number of issues such as ritual reciprocity which are of great interest to scholars like Tambiah and Yalman are not part of the focus of this monograph.

Finally, I would like to reiterate my hope that this study has succeeded in illuminating one of northern Thailand's most significant religious centers through a viable integration of interpretation and description by the use of a model which does justice to the richness and variety of the subject matter.

---

[1]Kenneth E. Wells, *Thai Buddhism* . . . , pp. 7ff.; Jane Bunnag, *Buddhist Monk, Buddhist Layman*, pp. 24 ff.; *Acts on the Administration of the Buddhist Order of Sangha* (Bangkok: Mahāmakuta Buddhist University, 1963).

[2]I have rendered *dek wat* as "lay student." Literally *dek wat* means "child of the *wat*." In most cases at a *wat* like Haripuñjaya these are students attending the Wat boys' school who are provided room and board for services of a housekeeping nature performed at the Wat. In particular they will assist monks in such activities as money transactions which are specifically forbidden the monk in the Vinaya.

[3]The following information about the abbot and his two assistants was supplied by them at my request. I am grateful for their warm cooperation.

[4]The *upajjhāya* (preceptor) is an officially designated monk responsible for instructing young men seeking ordination in the duties and responsibilities of monkhood. He is chosen by the ecclesiastical head of the province but the appointment is approved by the Supreme Sangha Council.

[5]See Jane Bunnag, *op. cit.*, p. 196; Kenneth E. Wells, *op. cit.*, p. 184.

[6]See Jane Bunnag, *op. cit.*, chap. II, for a discussion of the variety of tasks performed by the monk relative to the lay community.

[7]1973 figures provided by the Lamphun provincial Office of Education. Lamphun district figures corrected to 1974.

[8]Jane Bunnag, *op. cit.*, pp. 69ff.

[9]I am particularly indebted to Francis Seely for making available to me his charts and statistics on the organization of the Thai Sangha. Mr. Seely is currently completing a detailed handbook on Thai Buddhism.

[10]See Yoneo Ishii, "Church and State in Thailand," *Asian Survey*, vol. 8 (1968).

[11]Hans-Dieter Evers, *Monks, Priests and Peasants* (Leiden: E. J. Brill, 1972).

[12]For example, Michael Ames, "Magical-animism and Buddhism: A Structural Analysis of the Sinhalese Religious System," *Religion in South Asia*, ed. Edward Harper (Seattle: University of Washington Press, 1964); Gananath Obeyesekere, "The Buddhist Pantheon in Ceylon and Its Extensions," *Anthropological Studies in Theravada Buddhism*, ed. Manning Nash (New Haven: Yale University Southeast Asia Studies, 1966); Nur Yalman, "Dual Organization in Central Ceylon," *op. cit.*, ed. Manning Nash.

[13]See *Dhammaduta*, vol. 1 (Jan., Feb., March 1969).

[14]Report from the Wat Haripuñjaya magazine, *Santisukha* (July, 1974).

[15]Donald K. Swearer, "Community Development and Thai Buddhism, The Dynamics of Tradition and Change," *Visakha Puja 2516* (Bangkok: Buddhist Association, 1973), pp. 35-47. For a slightly different view, see Steven Piker, "Buddhism and Modernization in Contemporary Thailand," *Tradition and Change in Theravada Buddhism*, Contributions to Asian Studies, vol. 4 (Leiden: E. J. Brill, 1973), pp. 51-67.

[16]Charles E. Keyes, "Buddhism and National Integration in Thailand," *Journal of Asian Studies*, vol. XXX, no. 3 (May 1971).

[17]S. J. Tambiah, *op. cit.*, chap. 19.